Political Economy
Jean Charles Leonard Simonde de Sismondi

SAI Press
Dickinson, ND

ISBN-13: 978-1-105-46143-9

Political Economy

Jean Charles Leonard Simonde de Sismondi

Table of Contents

Chapter 1: Objects and Origins of the Science

Political economy is the name given to an important division of the science of government. The object of government is, or ought to be, the happiness of men, united in society; it seeks the means of securing to them the highest degree of felicity compatible with their nature, and at the same time of allowing the greatest possible number of individuals to partake in that felicity. But man is a complex bring; he experiences moral and physical wants; therefore his happiness consists in his moral and physical condition. The moral happiness of man, so far as it depends on his government, is intimately connected with the improvement of that government; it forms the object of civil policy, which ought to diffuse the happy influence of liberty, knowledge, virtue, and hope, over all classes of the community. Civil policy should point out the means of giving to nations a constitution, the liberty of which may elevate the souls of the citizens; an education which may form their hearts to virtue and open their minds to knowledge; a religion which may present to them the hopes of another life, to compensate for the sufferings of this. It should seek not what suits one man or one class of men, but what may impart most happiness by imparting most worth to all the men living under its laws.

The physical well-being of man, so far as it can be produced by his government, is the object of Political Economy. All the physical wants of man, for which he depends on his equals, are satisfied by means of wealth. It is this which commands labour, which purchases respectful service, which procures all that man has accumulated for use or pleasure. By means of it health is preserved, and life maintained; the wants of infancy and old age are supplied; food, and clothing, and shelter, are placed within the reach of all. Wealth may therefore be considered as representing all that men can do for the physical well-being of each other; and the science which shows to governments the true system of administering national wealth is an important branch of the science of national happiness.

Government is instituted for the advantage of all the Persons subject to it; hence it ought to keep the advantage of them all perpetually in view. And as in respect of civil policy it should extend to every citizen the benefits of liberty, virtue, and knowledge, so it ought likewise, in respect of political economy, to watch over all the advantages of the national fortune. Abstractly considered, the end of government is not to accumulate wealth in the state, but to make every citizen participate in those enjoyments of physical life which wealth represents. Government is called to second the work of providence, to augment the mass of felicity on earth and not to multiply the beings who live under its laws, faster than it can multiply their chances of happiness.

Wealth and population are not, indeed, absolute signs of prosperity in a state; they are only so in relation to each other. Wealth is a blessing when it spreads comfort over all classes; population is an advantage when every man is sure of gaining an honest subsistence by his labour. But a country may be wretched, though some individuals in it are amassing colossal fortunes; and if its population, like that of China, is always superior to its means of subsistence; if it is contented with living on the refuse of animals; if it is incessantly threatened with famine, this numerous population, far from being an object of envy, is a calamity.

The improvement of social order is generally advantageous to the poor as well as to the rich; and political economy points out the means of preserving this order by correction, but not of overturning it. It was a beneficent decree of Providence, which gave wants and sufferings to human nature; because out of these it has formed the incitements, which are to awaken our activity, and push us forward to develop our whole being. If we could succeed in excluding pain from the world, we must also exclude virtue; if we could banish want, we must also banish industry. Hence it is not the equality of ranks, but happiness in all ranks, which the legislator ought to have in view. It is not from the division of property that he will procure this happiness, but from labour and the reward of labour. It is by maintaining the activity and hopes of the mind; by securing to the poor man as well as to the rich, a regular subsistence and the sweets of life, in the performance of his task.

The title given by Adam Smith to his immortal work, on the science we are now engaged with, 'The Nature and Causes of the Wealth of Nations' forms at the same the most precise definition of that science. It presents a much more exact idea than the term political economy, afterwards adopted. The latter designation, at least, requires to be understood according to the modern acceptation of the word economy, not according to its etymology. In its present sense economy denotes the preservative, administrative, and the management of property; and it is because we use the somewhat tautological phrase domestic economy for the management of a private fortune, that we have come to use the phrase political economy for the management of the national fortune.

From the time when men first entered into social union, they must have occupied themselves with the common interests originating in their wealth. From the beginning of societies, a portion of the public wealth was set apart to provide for the public wants. The levying and management of this national revenue, which no longer pertained to each, became an essential part in the science of statesmen. It is what we call finance.

Private fortunes, on the other hand, made the interests of each citizen more complex; being exposed to the attacks of cupidity and fraud, their wealth required to be defended by the public authority, according to the fundamental article of the social contract, which had combined the strength of individuals to protect each with power of all. The rights over property, the divisions of it, the means of transmitting it, became one of the most important branches of civil jurisprudence; and the application of justice to the distribution of national property, formed an essential function of the legislator.

But no inquiry concerning the nature and causes of national wealth had occupied the speculations of our ancestors. They had not ascended to the principles of political economy, in order to deduce from that source their systems of finance and civil jurisprudence, which ought, however, to be nothing more than corollaries from those principles. They had abandoned the development of public wealth to the result of individual efforts, without examining their nature; and thus property had accumulated silently, in each society, by the labour of each artisan to procure his own subsistence, and afterwards his own comforts - before the manner of acquiring and preserving it became an object of scientific speculation. The philosophers of antiquity were engaged in proving to their disciples, that riches are useless for happiness; not in pointing out to governments the laws by which the increase of those riches may be favoured or retarded. The attention of thinking men was at length directed to national wealth by the requisitions of states, and the poverty of the people. An important change which occurred in the general politics of Europe, during the sixteenth century, almost every where overturned public liberty; oppressed the smaller states; destroyed the privileges of the towns and provinces; and conferred the right to dispose of national fortunes on a small number of sovereigns, absolutely unacquainted with the industry by which wealth is accumulated or preserved. Before the reign of Charles V, one half of Europe, lying under the feudal system, had no liberty or knowledge, and no finance. But the other half, which had already reached a high degree of prosperity, which was daily increasing its agricultural riches, its manufactories, and its trade, was governed by men who, in private life, had attended to the study of economy, when, in acquiring their own property, had learned what is suitable in that of states; and who, governing free communities to which they were responsible, guided their administrations, not according to their own ambition, but according to the interest of all. Till the fifteenth century wealth and credit were no where to be found in the republics of Italy, and of the Hanseatic league; the imperial towns of Germany; the free towns of Belgium and Spain, and perhaps also in some towns in France and England, which happened to enjoy great municipal privileges. The Magistrates of all those towns were men constantly brought up in business, and without having brought political economy to the form of a science, they had yet the feeling as well as the experience of what would serve or injure the interests of their fellow-citizens.

The dreadful wars which began with the nineteenth century, and altogether overturned the balance of Europe, transferred a nearly absolute monarchy to three or four all-powerful monarchs, who shared among them the government of the civilized world. Charles V united, under his dominion, all the counties which had hitherto been celebrated for their industry and wealth, - Spain, nearly all Italy, Flanders, and Germany; but he united after having ruined them; and his administration, by suppressing all their privileges, prevented the recovery of former opulence. The most absolute kings can no more govern by themselves, than kings whose authority is limited by laws. The former transmit their power to ministers whom they themselves select, in place of taking such as would be nominated by the popular confidence. But they find them among a class of persons different from that in which free governments find them. In the eyes of an absolute king, the first quality of a statesman is his being in possession of a rank so high that he may have lived in noble indolence, or at least in absolute ignorance of domestic economy. The ministers of Charles V, whatever talents they show for negotiation and intrigue, were all equally ignorant of pecuniary affairs. They ruined the public finances, agriculture, trade, and every kind of industry, from one end of Europe to the other; they made the people feel the difference, which might indeed have been anticipated, between their ignorance and the practical

11

knowledge of republican magistrates.

Charles V, his rival Francis I, and Henry VIII, who wished to hold the balance between them, had engaged in expenses beyond their incomes; the ambition nf their successors, and the obstinacy of the house of Austria, which continued to maintain a destructive system of warfare during more than a hundred years, caused those expenses, in spite of the public poverty, to go on increasing. But as the suffering became more general, the friends of humanity felt more deeply the obligation laid on them to undertake the defence of the poor. By an order of sequence opposite to the natural progress of ideas, the science of political economy sprung from that of finance. Philosophers wished to shield the people from the speculations of absolute power. They felt that, to obtain a hearing from kings, they must speak to them of royal interests, not of justice or duty. They investigated the nature and causes of national wealth, to show governments how it might be shared without being destroyed.

Too little liberty existed in Europe to allow those who first occupied themselves with political economy to present their speculations to the world; and finances were enveloped in too profound a secrecy to admit of men, not engaged in public business, knowing facts enough to form the basis of general rules. Hence the study of political economy began with ministers, when once it had fortunately happened that kings put men at the head of their finances, who combined talents with justice and love of the public weal. Two great French ministers, Sully under Henry IV, and Colbert under Louis XIV, were the first who threw any light on a subject till then regarded as a secret of state, in which mystery had engendered and concealed the greatest absurdities. Yet, in spite of all their genius and authority, it was a task beyond their power to introduce any thing like order, precision, or uniformity into this branch of government. Both of them, however, not only repressed the frightful spoliations of the revenue farmers, and by their protection communicated some degree of security to private fortunes; but likewise dimly perceived the true sources of national prosperity, and busied themselves with efforts to make them flow more abundantly. Sully gave his chief protection to agriculture. He used to say that pasturage and husbandry wee the two beasts of the state. Colbert, descended from a family engaged in the cloth trade, studied above all to encourage manufactures and commerce. He furnished himself with the opinion of merchants, and asked their advice on all emergencies. Both statesmen opened roads and canals to facilitate the exchange of commodities: both protected the spirit of enterprise, and honoured the industrious activity which diffused plenty over their country.

Colbert, the latter of the two, was greatly prior to any of the writers who have teated political economy as a science, and reduced it to a body of doctrines. He had a system, however, in regard to national wealth: he required one to give uniformity to his plans, and delineate clearly before his view the object he wished to attain. His system was probably suggested by the merchants whom he consulted. It is now generally known by the epithet mercantile, sometimes also by the name Colbertism. Not that Colbert was its author, or unfolded it in any publication; but because he was beyond comparison the most illustrious of its professors; because, notwithstanding the errors of his theory, the applications he deduced from it were highly advantageous; and because, among the numerous writers who have maintained the same opinion, there is not one who has shown enough of talent even to fix his name in the reader's memory. It is but just, however, to separate the mercantile system altogether from the name of Colbert. It was a system invented by trading subjects, not by citizens; it was a system adopted by all the ministers of absolute governments, when they happened to take the trouble of thinking on finance, and Colbert had no other share in the matter than that of having followed it without reforming it.

After long treating commerce with haughty contempt, governments had at length discovered in it one of the most abundant sources of national wealth. All the great fortunes in their states did not indeed belong exclusively to merchants; but when, overtaken by sudden necessity, they wished to levy large sums at once, merchants alone could supply them. Proprietors of land might possess immense revenues, manufacturers might cause immense labours to be executed; but neither of them could dispose of any more than their income or annual produce. In a case of need merchants alone offered their whole fortune to the government. As their capital was entirely represented by commodities already prepared for consumption, by merchandise destined for the immediate use of the market to which it had been carried, they could sell it at an hour's warning, and realise the required sum with smaller loss than any other class of citizens. Merchants therefore found means to make themselves be listened to, because they had in some sort the command of all the money in the state, and were at the same time nearly independent of authority - being able, in general, to hide from the attacks of despotism a property of unknown amount, and transport it, with their persons, to a foreign country, at a moment's notice.

Governments would gladly have increased the merchant's profit, on condition of obtaining a share of it. Imagining that nothing more was necessary than to second each other's views, they offered him force to support industry. and since the advantage of the merchant consists in selling dear and buying cheap, they thought it would be an effectual protection to commerce, if the means were afforded of selling still dearer and buying still cheaper. The merchants whom they consulted eagerly grasped at this proposal; and thus was founded the mercantile system. Antonio de Leyva, Fernando de Gonnzago, and the Duke of Alva, viceroys of Charles V and his descendants - the rapacious inventors of so many monopolies - had no other notion of political economy. But when it was attempted to reduce this methodical robbery of consumers into a system; when deliberative assemblies were occupied with it; when Colbert consulted corporations; when the people at last began to perceive the true state of the case, it became necessary to find out a more honourable basis for such transactions; it became necessary not only to study the advantage of financiers and merchants, but also that of the nation: for the calculations of self-interest cannot show themselves in open day, and the first benefit of publicity is to impose silence on base sentiments.

Under these circumstances the mercantile system was moulded into a plausible form; and doubtless it must have been plausible, since, even till our own times, it continued to seduce the greater part of practical men employed in trade and finance. Wealth, said those earliest economists, is money: the two words were received into universal use as almost entirely synonymous; no one dreamed of questioning the identity of money and wealth. Money, they said, disposes of men's labour and of all its fruits. It is money which produces those fruits; it is by means of money that industry continues in a nation; to its influence each individual owes his subsistence and the continuation of his life. Money is especially necessary in the relation of one state to another. It supports war and forms the strength of armies. The state which has it, rules over that which has it not. The whole science of political economy ought, therefore, to have for its object the increase of money in a nation. But the money possessed by a nation cannot be augmented in quantity, except by the working of mines, if the nation has any; or by foreign trade, if it has none. All the exchanges carried on within a country, all the purchases and sales which take place among Englishmen, for instance, do not increase the specie contained within the shores of England by a single penny. Hence it is necessary to And means of importing money from other countries; and trade alone can do this by selling much to foreigners and buying little from them. For in the same way as each merchant in settling with his correspondent, sees at the year's end whether he has sold more than he has bought, and Ands himself accordingly creditor or debtor by a balance account which must be paid in money; so likewise a nation, by summing up all its purchases and all its sales with each nation, or with all together, would find itself every year creditor or

15

debtor by a commercial balance which must be paid in money. If the country pay this balance, it will constantly grow poorer; if it receive the balance, it will constantly grow richer.

For a century, the mercantile system was universally adopted by cabinets; universally favoured by traders and chambers of commerce; universally expounded by writers, as if it had been proved by the most unexceptionable demonstration, no one deeming it worth while to establish it by new proofs; when, after the middle of the eighteenth century, Quesnay opposed to it his Tableau Economique, afterwards expounded by Mirabeau and the Abbe de Riviere, enlarged by Dupont de Nemours, and adopted by a numerous sect which arose in France, under the name of Economists. In Italy too this sect gained some distinguished partisans. Its followers have written more about the science than those of any other sect; yet they have admitted Quesnay's principles with such blind confidence, and maintained them with such implicit fidelity, that one is at a loss to discover any difference of principle, or any progress of ideas in their several productions.

Thus Quesnay founded a second system in political economy, still named the territorial system, or more precisely the system of the economists. He begins by asserting that gold and silver, the signs of wealth, the means of exchange, the price of all commodities, do not themselves constitute the wealth of states; and that no judgment can be formed concerning the prosperity of a nation, from the abundance of its precious metals. He next proceeds to survey the different classes of men, all of whom, occupied in gaining money, and causing wealth to circulate, even when acquiring it for themselves, are not, according to him, occupied with any thing besides exchange. He endeavours to distinguish the classes possessed of a creative power; it is amongst them that wealth must originate, all the transactions of commerce appearing to be nothing else but the transmission of that wealth from hand to hand.

The merchant who carries the productions of both

hemispheres from one continent to the other, and on returning to the ports of his own country, obtains, at the sale of his cargo, a sum double of that with which he began his voyage, does not, after all, appear, in the eyes of Quesnay, to have performed any thing but an exchange. If, in the colonies, he has sold the manufactures of Europe at a higher price than they cost him, the reason is, they were in fact worth more. Together with their prime cost, he must also be reimbursed for the value of his time, his cares, his subsistence, and that of his sailors and agents during the voyage. He has a like reimbursement to claim on the cotton or sugar he brings back to Europe. If, at the end of his voyage, any profit remains, it is the fruit of his economy and good management. The wages allowed him by consumers, for the trouble he has undergone, are greater than the sum he had expended. It is the nature of wages, however, to be entirely expended by him who earns them; and had this merchant done so, he would have added nothing to the national wealth, by the labour of his whole life; because the produce which he brings back does nothing more than exactly replace the valuE of the produce given for it, added to his own wages, and the wages of all that were engaged with him in the business.

Agreeably to this reasoning, the French philosopher gave to transport trade the name of economical trade, which it still retains. This species of commerce, he asserts, is not destined to provide for the wants of the nation that engages in it, but merely to serve the convenience of two foreign nations. The carrying nation acquires from it no other profit than wages, and cannot grow rich except by the saving which economy enables it to make on them.

Quesnay, next adverting to manufactures, considers them an exchange, just the same as commerce; but instead of having in view two present values, their primitive contract is, in his opinion, an exchange of the present against the future. The merchandise produced by the labour of the artisan is but the equivalent of his accumulated wages. During his labour, he had consumed the fruits of the earth, and the work produced by him

17

is nothing but their value.

The economist next directs his attention to agriculture. The labourer appears to him to be in the same condition as the merchant and the artisan. Like the latter, he makes with the earth an exchange of the present against the future. The crops produced by him represent the accumulated value of his labour; they pay his hire, to which he has the same right as the artisan to his wages, or the merchant to his profit. But when this hire has been deducted, there remains a net revenue, which was not be found in manufactures and commerce; it is what the labourer pays the proprietor for the use of his land. This revenue, Quesnay thinks, is of a nature quite different from any other. It is not wages; it is not the result of an exchange; it is the price of the earth's spontaneous labour, the fruit of nature's beneficence; and since it does not represent pre-existent wealth, it alone must be the source of every kind of wealth. Tracing the value of all other commodities, under all its transformations, Quesnay still discovers its first origin in the fruits of the earth. The labours of the husbandman, of the artisan, of the merchant, consume those fruits in the shape of wages and produce them under new forms. The proprietor alone receives them at their source from the hands of nature herself, and by means of them is enabled to pay the wages of all his countrymen, who labour only for him.

This ingenious system totally supplanted that of the merchants. The economists denied the existence of that commercial balance to which their antagonists attached so much importance; they asserted the impossibility of that accumulation of gold and silver which the others expected from it; throughout the nation, they could see only proprietors of land, the sole dispensers of the national fortune; productive workmen, or labourers producing the revenue of the former. and a hired class, in which they ranked merchants also denying to them, as to the artisans, the faculty of producing any thing.

The plans, which these two sects recommended to governments, differed not less than their principles. While the mercantilists wished authority to interfere in every thing, the economists incessantly repeated laissez faire et laissez passer (let every man do as he pleases, and every thing take its course;) for as the public interest consists in the union of all individual interests, individual interest will guide each man more surely to the public interest than any government can do.

An excessive ferment was excited in France by the system of the economists. The government of that nation allowed the people to talk about public affairs, but not to understand them. The discussion, of Quesnay's theory was sufficiently unshackled; but none of the facts or documents in the hands of the administration, were presented to the public eye. In the system of the French economists, it is easy to discern the effects produced by this mixture of ingenious theory and involuntary ignorance. It seduced the people, because they were now for the first time occupied with their own public affairs. But, during these discussions, a free nation, possessed of the right to examine its own public affairs, was producing a system not less ingenious, and much better supported by fact and observation; a system which, after a short struggle, at length cast its predecessors into the shade; for truth always triumphs in the end, over dreams, however brilliant.

Adam Smith, author of this third system, which represents labour as the sole origin of wealth, and economy as the sole means of accumulating it, has, in one sense, carried the science of political economy to perfection, at a single step. Experience, no doubt, has disclosed new truths to us; the experience of late years, in particular, has forced us to make sad discoveries: but in completing the system of Smith, that experience has also confirmed it. Of the various succeeding authors, no one has sought any other theory. Some have applied what he advanced to the administration of different counties; others have confirmed it by new experiments and new observations; some have expanded it by developments, which flow from the principles laid down by him; some have even here and there detected errors in his work; but it has been by following out the truths which he taught and rectifying them by light borrowed from its author. Never did philosopher effect a more complete revolution in any science: for those even who dissent from his doctrine acknowledge his authority; sometimes they attack, solely because they do not understand him; most commonly, they flatter themselves with the belief of still following, even while they contradict him. We shall devote the rest of this article to explain the science which he taught us, though in an order different from his. We shall arrange it under the six following heads: Formation and Progress of Wealth: Territorial Wealth; Commercial Wealth; Money; Taxes; and Population.

Chapter 2: Formation and Progress of Wealth

Man brings into the world with him certain wants, which he must satisfy in order to live; certain desires which lead him to expect happiness from particular enjoyments; and a certain industry or aptitude for labour, which enables him to satisfy the requisitions of both. His wealth originates in this industry: his wants and desires are its employments. All that man values is created by his industry; all that he creates is destined to be consumed in satisfying his wants and desires. But, between the moment of its production by labour, and its consumption by enjoyment, the thing destined for man's use may have an existence more or less durable. It is this thing, this accumulated and still unconsumed fruit of labour, which is called wealth.

Wealth may exist not only without any sign of exchange, or without money, but even without any possibility of exchange, or without trade. Suppose a man to be left on a desert island; the undisputed property of this whole island is not wealth, whatever be the natural fertility of its soil, the abundance of the game straying in its forests, of the fish sporting on its shores, or the mines concealed in its bosom. On the contrary, amid all these benefits presented him by nature, the man may sink to the lowest degree of penury, and die perhaps of hunger. But, if his industry enables him to catch some of the animals that wander in his woods: and if, instead of consuming them immediately, he reserves them for his future wants; if, in this interval, he gets them tamed and multiplied, so that he can live on their milk, or associate them to his labour, he is then beginning to acquire wealth, because labour has gained him the possession of these animals, and a fresh labour has rendered them domestic. The measure of his wealth will not be the price, which he might obtain for his property in exchange, because he is debarred from all exchange, but the length of time during which no farther labour will be requisite to satisfy his wants, compared with the extent of those wants.

By subduing those animals, the man has made them his property and wealth; by subduing the ground, he will, in like manner, convert it into property and wealth. His island is destitute of value so long as no labour has been bestowed on it; but if, instead of consuming its fruits the moment they come to his hand, he reserves them for future want; if he commits them again to the earth, again to be multiplied; if he tills his fields to augment their productive power, or defends them by inclosures from wild beasts; if he plants them with trees, the fruit of which he does not look for till many years have elapsed; he is then creating the value, not only of annual produce raised by his labour from the ground, but also of the ground itself, which he had tamed, as he tamed the wild beasts, and rendered fit to second his exertions. In that case he is rich, and the more so the longer he can suspend his labours without suffering new wants.

Our Solitary, being now liberated from the most pressing of all demands, that of hunger, may devote his exertions to provide lodging and clothes, or to improve those already provided. He will build himself a hut, and fit it out with such furniture as his unaided labour may suffice to construct; he will change the skin and fleeces of his sheep into shoes or coats; and the more convenient his dwelling shall be rendered, the better his storehouse shall be filled with provision for his future food and clothing, the more rich may he call himself.

The history of this man is the history of the human race: labour alone has created all kinds of wealth. However great the beneficence of nature, she gives nothing gratuitously to man; though, when addressed by him, she is ready to lend her assistance in multiplying his powers to an indefinite extent. The history of wealth is, in all cases, comprised within the limits now specified - the labour which creates, the economy which accumulates, the consumption which destroys. An article which has not been wrought, or has not mediately or immediately received its value from labour, is not wealth, however useful, however necessary, it may be for life. An article, which is not useful to man, which does not satisfy any of his desires, and

22

cannot mediately or immediately be employed in his service, is not more entitled to the name of wealth, whatever labour may have been bestowed on producing it. And finally, an article which cannot be accumulated or kept for future consumption is not wealth, though created by labour and consumed by enjoyment.

Before possessing any medium of exchange, before discovering the precious metals which render it so easy to us, our Solitary would ere long learn to distinguish the different kinds of labour in their relation to wealth. Labour producing no enjoyment is useless; labour, whose fruits are naturally incapable of being stored up for future consumption, is unproductive; whilst the only productive kinds of labour - the only kinds producing wealth - are such as leave behind them, in the estimation even of our Solitary, a pledge equal in value to the trouble they have cost. Thus the man, misled by analogy, may have imagined that he could multiply his olive-trees by planting the olives; he may not have known but that the stones would germinate as in other such vegetables; till, after preparing the ground by a complete and fatiguing tillage, experience would teach him that his toil had been useless, for no olive-tree was produced by it. On the other hand, he may have secured his dwelling from wolves and bears; and the labour would be useful but unproductive; for its fruits cannot accumulate. If previously accustomed to civilized life, he may have passed many hours in playing on a flute, saved, we shall suppose, at his shipwreck; the labour would still be useful, and probably regarded as his own pleasure; but it would be as unproductive, and for a like reason, as before. He may have bestowed on the care of his person and health much time, very usefully employed; this will also be quite unproductive of wealth. The Solitary will clearly perceive what difference there is between productive labour and the labour of hours in which he amasses nothing for the future; and, without excluding himself from such occupations, he will call them a loss of time.

Whatever holds of the isolated man, with regard to

creating and preserving wealth, is true also of society, - when labour, shared among numerous individuals, is recompensed by wages, while its fruits are distributed by exchange. For the society, as well as for the Solitary, there may be a useless as well as an unproductive kind of labour; and, though both of them be paid, they still preserve their distinct character, since the first corresponds not to the desires or wants of the labourer's employer, and the second admits no accumulation of its fruits. The wage paid to the workmen in either case must not mislead us; it puts the payer of it in the workman's place. The part which we formerly supposed to be performed by a single individual, is now shared among two or more persons; but the result is not altered in the least. The day-labourer who plants olives performs a task which is useless to his employer, though, if he receives his hire, it may be advantageous to himself. The man who defends his master or society against bears or hostile enterprises; who takes charge of the health or the persons of others; who provides the enjoyment of music, or dramatic exhibition, or dancing, performs, just like the Solitary, a work which is useful because it is agreeable, which is lucrative to him because he receives a hire for his labour, whilst he abandons the enjoyment of it to his employers; but which is unproductive notwithstanding, because it cannot be the object of saving and accumulation. He who paid the wage, no longer has either the wage itself in his possession, or the thing for which he gave it.

Thus labour and economy - the true sources of wealth - exist for the Solitary as well as for the social man, and produce the same kind of advantage to both. The formation of society, however, and with it the introduction of commerce and exchange, were necessary both to augment the productive power of labour, by dividing it, and to afford a more precise aim to economy, by multiplying the enjoyments which wealth procures. Thus men, combined in society, produced more than if each had laboured separately; and they preserve better what they have produced, because they feel the value of it better.

Exchange first arose from superabundance: "Give me

that article, which is of no service to you, and would be useful to me,,, said one of the contacting parties, "and I will give you this in return, which is of no service to me, and would be useful to you." Present utility was not, however, the sole measure of things exchanged. Each estimated for himself the selling price, or the trouble and time bestowed in the production of his own commodity, and compared it with the buying price, or the trouble and time necessary for procuring the required commodity by his own efforts; and no exchange could take place till the two contacting parties, on calculating the matter, had each discovered that it was better thus to procure the commodity wanted than to make it for himself. This accidental advantage soon pointed out to both a constant source of advantage in trading, whenever the one offered an article which he excelled in making, for an article which the other excelled in making; for each excelled in what he made often, each was unskillful and slow at what he made but seldom. Now, the more exclusively they devoted themselves to one kind of work, the more dexterity did they acquire in it, the more effectually did they succeed in rendering it easy and expeditious. This observation produced the division of trades; the husbandman quickly perceived, that he could not make as many agricultural tools by himself, in a month, as the blacksmith would make for him in a day.

The same principle which at first separated the trades of the husbandman, shepherd, smith, and weaver, continued to separate those trades into an indefinite number of departments. Each felt that, by simplifying the operation committed to him, he would perform it in a manner still more speedy and perfect. The weaver renounced the business of spinning and dyeing; the spinning of hemp, cotton, wool, and silk, became each separate employment; weavers were still farther subdivided, according to the fabric and the destination of their stuffs; and at every subdivision, each workman, directing his attention to a single object, experienced an increase in his productive powers. In the interior of each manufactory, this division was again repeated, and still with the same success. Twenty workmen all laboured at the same thing, but each made it undergo a different operation: and the twenty workmen found that they had accomplished twenty times as much work as when each had laboured separately.

Much more work was executed in the world by the division of labour; but, at the same time, much more was required to supply the consumption. The wants and the enjoyments of the Solitary, who laboured for himself, were both very limited. Food, clothing, and lodging, he indeed required; but he did not so much as think of the delicacies, by which the satisfaction of those wants might be converted into pleasure; and still less of the artificial desires, induced by society, which in their gratification become new sources of enjoyment. The Solitary's aim was merely to amass, that he might afterwards repose. Before him at no great distance, was a point in the accumulation of wealth, beyond which it would have been foolishness to accumulate more, because his consumption could not be increased proportionably. But the wants of the social man were infinite, because the society's labour offered him enjoyment infinitely varied. Whatever wealth he might amass, he could never have occasion to say it is enough; he still found means to convert it into pleasure, and to imagine at least that he applied it to his service.

Trade, the generic name given to the total mass of exchangers, complicated the relation required to subsist between production and consumption; yet far from diminishing, it increased its importance. At first, every one procured what he himself intended to consume; but when each had come to work for all, the production of all must be consumed by all; and each, in what he produced, must have an eye to the final demand of the society, for which he destined the fruit of his labour. This demand, though not well ascertained by him, was limited in quantity. for, in order to continue his expenditure, every one must confine it by certain restrictions, and the sum of those private expenditures constituted that of the society. The distinction between capital and income, which in the Solitary's case was still confused, became essential in society. The social man was under the necessity of adjusting his consumption to his income, and the society, of which he formed part, were compelled to observe the same rule; without incurring ruin, they could not annually consume more than their annual income, leaving their capital untouched. All that they produced, however, was destined for consumption; and if their annual products, when carried to the destined market, found no purchaser, reproduction was arrested, and the nation ruined as before. We shall attempt to explain this double relation, at once so essential and so delicate, by showing, on the one hand, how income springs from capital; on the other, how what is income for one may be capital for a second.

To the Solitary, every kind of wealth was a provision made beforehand against the moment of necessity; yet still in this provision he distinguished two things - the part which it suited his economy to keep in reserve for immediate, or nearly immediate use, and the part which he would not need before the time when he might obtain it by a new production. One portion of his corn was to support him till the next harvest; another portion, set apart for seed, was to bring forth its fruit the following year.

The formation of society, the introduction of exchange, allowed him almost indefinitely to multiply this seed, - this fruit-bearing portion of accumulated wealth. It is what we name capital.

The ground and his animals were all that man could force to work in concert with him; but, in society, the rich man could force the poor to work in concert with him. After having set apart what corn was necessary till the next harvest, it suited him to employ the remaining surplus of corn in feeding other men, that they might cultivate the ground and make fresh corn for him: that they might spin and weave his hemps and wools; that, in a word, they might take out of his hands the commodity ready for being consumed, and at the expiration of a certain period, return him another commodity, of a greater value, likewise destined for consumption. Wages were the price at which the rich man obtained the poor man's labour in exchange. The division of labour had produced the distinction of ranks. The person who had limited his efforts to perform only one very simple operation in a manufacture, had made himself dependent on whoever chose to employ him. He no longer produced a complete work, but merely the part of a work; in which he required not only the cooperation of other workmen, but also raw materials, proper implements, and a trader to undertake the exchange of the article which he had contributed to finish. Whenever he bargained with a master-workman for the exchange of labour against subsistence, the condition he stood in was always disadvantageous, since his need of subsistence and his inability to procure it of himself, were far greater than the master's need of labour; and therefore he almost constantly narrowed his demand to bare necessaries, without which the stipulated labour could not have proceeded; whilst the master alone profited from the increase of productive power brought about by the division of labour.

The master, who hired workmen, was situated, in all points, exactly as the husbandman who sows the ground. The wages paid to his workmen were a kind of seed which he entrusted to them, and expected in a given time to bring forth fruit. Like the husbandman, he did not sow all his productive wealth; a part of it had been devoted to such buildings, or machines, or implements, as make labour more easy and productive; just in the way that a part of the husbandman's wealth was devoted to permanent works, destined to render the ground more fertile. It is thus that we see the different kinds of wealth springing up and separating, whilst each exerts a different influence on its own reproduction. The funds of consumption, such as domestic necessaries, do not any longer produce fruit, after each has secured them for his own use; fixed capital, such as improvement of the soil, canals of irrigation, and machinery, during the progress of its own slow consumption, co-operates with labour of which it augments the products; and, lastly, circulating capital, such as seed, wages, and raw materials, destined to be wrought, is consumed annually, or even more rapidly, in order to be again re-produced. It is essentially important to remark, that those three kinds of wealth are all equally advancing towards consumption. But the first when consumed is absolutely destroyed; for societies, as for individuals, it is merely an expense: whereas the second and third, after being consumed, are re-produced under a new form; and for societies, as for individuals, the consumption of them is a putting out to profit, or the circulation of capitals.

We shall better understand this movement of wealth, which, perhaps, it is difficult to follow, by fixing our observation on a single family engaged in the simplest of all speculations. A solitary farmer has reaped a hundred bags of corn, and is destitute of any market to which he can carry it. At all events, this corn must be consumed within the year, otherwise it will be worth nothing to the farmer. But he and his family may require only thirty bags of it; this is his expense: another thirty may be employed to support workmen engaged in felling the forests, or draining the marshes of the neighbourhood, to put them under culture; this will be converting thirty bags into fixed capital: and, finally, the remaining forty bags may be sown, and formed into a circulating capital, in place of the twenty bags sown the preceding year. The hundred are thus consumed; but seventy of them are put out to profit, they will reappear partly at the next harvest, partly at those which follow. By this means, in consuming he will have saved. Yet the limits of such an operation are easily discerned. If, this year, out of the hundred bags which he reaped, he could get no more than sixty eaten, who will eat the two hundred bags produced next year by the augmentation of his seed?*

Resuming these three sorts of wealth, which, as we have seen, become distinct in a private family, let us now consider each sort with regard to the whole nation, and see how the national revenue may arise from this division.

As the farmer required a primitive quantity of labour to be expended in cutting down the forests, and draining the marshes which he meant to cultivate; so, for every kind of enterprise, there is required a primitive quantity of labour to facilitate and augment the circulating capital. The ore cannot be obtained till the mine is opened; canals must be dug, machinery and mills must be constructed, before they can be used; manufactories must be built, and looms set up, before the wool, the hemp, or the silk can be weaved. This first advance is always accomplished by labour; this labour is always represented by wages; and these wages are always exchanged for necessaries of life, which the workmen consume in executing their task. Hence what we have called fixed capital, is a part of the annual consumption, transformed into durable establishments, calculated to increase the productive power of future labour. Such establishments themselves grow old, decay, and are slowly consumed in their turn, after having long contributed to augment the annual production.

As the farmer required seed, which, after being committed to the earth, was returned fivefold in harvest; so likewise, every undertaker of useful labour requires raw materials to work upon, and wages for his workmen, equivalent to the necessaries of life consumed by them in their labour. His operations thus begin with a consumption; and this is followed by a reproduction which should be more abundant, since it must be equivalent to the raw materials worked upon, so the necessaries of life consumed by his workmen in their labour, to the sum by which his machinery and all his fixed capitals have been deteriorated during the production, and lastly to the profit of all concerned in the labour, who have supported its fatigues solely in the hope of gaining by it. The farmer sowed twenty bags of corn to reap a hundred; the manufacturer will make a calculation nearly similar. And as the farmer at harvest must recover not only a compensation for his seed, but likewise for

30

all his labours, so the manufacturer must find in his production, not the raw materials only, but all the wages of his workmen, all the interests and profits of his fixed capital, with all the interests and profits of his circulating capital.

In the last place, the farmer may augment his seed every year; but he will not fail to recollect that, since his crops increase in the same necessaries, he is not sure of always finding men to eat them. The manufacturer, in like manner, devoting the savings of each year to increase his re-production, must recollect the necessity of finding purchasers and consumers for the increasing products of his establishment.

Since the fund destined for consumption no longer produces any thing, and since each man strives incessantly to preserve and augment his fortune, each will also restrict his consumable fund, and instead of accumulating in his house a quantity of necessaries greatly superior to what he can consume, he will augment his fixed or circulating capital, by all that he does not expend. In the present condition of society, a part of the fund destined for consumption remains in the retail-dealer's hand, awaiting the buyer's confidence; another part destined to be consumed very slowly, as houses, furniture, carriages, horses, continues in the hands of persons whose business it is to sell the use of it, without abandoning the property. A considerable portion of the wealth of opulent nations is constantly thrown back into the fields destined for consumption; but although it still gives profit to its holders, it has ceased to augment the national re-production.

The annual distribution of the wealth, annually reproduced, among all the citizens composing the nation, constitutes the national revenue. It consists of all the value, by which the re-production surpasses the consumption that produced it. Thus the farmer, after deducting from his crop a quantity equal to the seed of the foregoing year, finds remaining the part which is to support his family, - a revenue to which they have acquired right by means of their annual labour; the part which is to support his workmen, who have acquired the right to it by the same title; the part with which he is to satisfy the landlord, who has acquired right to this revenue by the original improvement of the soil, now no longer repeated; and lastly, the part with which he is to pay the interest of his debts, or indemnify himself for the employment of his own capital - a revenue to which he has acquired right by the primitive labours which produced his capital.

So likewise, the manufacturer finds, in the annual produce of his manufactory, first the raw material employed; secondly, the equivalent of his own wages, and those of his workmen, to which their labour alone gives them right; thirdly, an equivalent for the annual detriment and interest of his fixed capital, to which revenue he or the proprietor has acquired right by a primitive labour; and lastly, an equivalent for the interest of his circulating capital, which has been produced by another primitive labour.

It is to be observed that, among those who share the national revenue, some acquire a new right in it every year by a new labour, others have previously acquired a permanent right by a primitive labour, which has rendered the annual labour more advantageous. No one obtains a share of the national revenue, except in virtue of what he himself or his representatives have accomplished to produce it; unless, as we shall soon see, he receives it at second hand, from its primitive proprietors, by way of compensation for services done to them. Now, whoever consumes without fulfilling the condition which alone gives him right to the revenue; whoever consumes without having a revenue, or beyond what he has; whoever consumes his capital in place of revenue, is advancing to ruin; and a nation composed of such consumers is advancing to ruin likewise. Revenue, indeed, is that quantity by which the national wealth is increased every year, and which accordingly may be destroyed, without the nation's becoming poorer; but the nation which, without re-production, destroys a quantity of wealth, superior in this annual increase, destroys the very means by which it would have acquired an equal re-production in subsequent years.

By a circular concatenation, in which every effect becomes a cause in its turn, production gives revenue, revenue furnishes and regulates a consumable fund, which fund again causes production and measures it. The national wealth continues to augment, and the state to prosper, so long as these three quantities, which are proportional to each other, continue to augment in a gradual manner, but whenever the proportion among them is broken, the state decays. A derangement of the mutual proportion subsisting among production, revenue, and consumption, becomes equally prejudicial to the nation, whether the production give a revenue smaller than usual, in which case a part of the capital must pass to the fund of consumption; or whether, on the contrary, this consumption diminish, and no longer call for a fresh production. To cause distress in the state, it is enough that the equilibrium be broken. Production may diminish when habits of idleness gain footing among the labouring classes; capital may diminish when prodigality and luxury become fashionable; and lastly, consumption may diminish from causes of poverty, unconnected with the diminution of labour, and yet, as it will not offer employment for future re-production, it must diminish labour in its turn.

Thus nations incur dangers that seem incompatible: they fall into ruin equally by spending too much, and by spending too little. A nation spends too much whenever it exceeds its revenue, because it cannot do so except by encroaching on its capital, and thus diminishing future production; it then does what the solitary cultivator would do if he should eat the corn which ought to be secured for seed. A nation spends too little, whenever, being destitute of foreign commerce, it does not consume its own production; or when, enjoying foreign commerce, it does not consume the excess of its production above its exportation; for, if so, it soon comes into the condition of the solitary cultivator, who having filled all his granaries far

33

beyond the probability of consumption, would be obliged, that he might not work in vain, partly to abandon his cultivation of the ground.

The nation does not indeed spend all that it consumes; the name expenditure, in such a case, can properly be given to that consumption only which produces nothing; while that part of the consumption which represents the wages of productive workmen, is an employment of funds, not an expenditure. Thus, the nation, when it forms manufacturing establishments, does not diminish its consumption; it consumes, in a productive manner, what it formerly consumed unproductively. Still, however, this employment of the national produce in giving movement to new labour, though it does not destroy the balance between production and consumption, renders it much more complex. The new produce thus obtained must, at last, find a consumer; and though it may be generally affirmed, that to increase the labour is to increase the wealth, and with it in a similar proportion the revenue and the consumption; still it is any thing but proved, that by too rapid an increase of its labour a nation may not altogether deviate from the proper rate of consumption, and thus ruin itself by economy as well as prodigality. Happily, in most cases, the increase of capital, of revenue and of consumption, requires no superintendence; they proceed, of their own accord, with an equal pace; and when one of them, at any time, happens to pass the others for an instant, foreign commerce is almost always ready to restore the equilibrium.

We have designedly carried on our history of the formation and progress of wealth thus far, without mentioning a circulating medium, to show, that, in fact, such an instrument is not necessary for its development. A circulating medium did not create wealth; but it simplified all the relations, and facilitated all the transactions of commerce; it gave to each the means of finding sooner what suited him best; and thus presenting an advantage to every one, it still further increased the wealth, which was already increasing without it.

The precious metals are one of the numerous values produced by the labour of man, and applicable to his use. It was soon discovered that they, more than any other species of riches, possessed the property of being preserved without alteration for any length of time, and the no less valuable one of uniting easily into a single whole, after being divided almost infinitely. The two halves of a piece of cloth, of a fleece, and still less of an ox, - though these are supposed to have once been employed as money, - were not worth the whole; but the two halves, the four quarters of a pound of gold are always, and will be, a pound of gold, however long they may be kept. As the first exchange of which men feel the need, is that which enables them to preserve the fruit of their labour for a future season, every one became eager to get precious metals in exchange for his commodity, whatever it might be; not because he at all intended to use those metals himself; but because he was sure of being able to exchange them at any time afterwards, in the same manner, and for the same reason, against whatever article he might then need. From that time the precious metals began to he sought after, not that they might be employed in the use of man, as ornaments or utensils, but that they might be accumulated, at first, as representing every species of wealth, and then that they might be used in commerce, as the means of facilitating all kinds of exchange.

Gold dust, in its primitive state, continues, even now, to be the medium of exchange among the African nations. But when once the value of gold comes to be universally admitted, there remains but a single step, much easier and far less important, till it be converted into coin, which warrants, by a legal stamp, the weight and the fineness of every particle of the precious metals employed in circulation.

The invention of money gave quite a new activity to exchange. Whoever happened to possess any superfluity had no longer occasion to seek the article likely to be needed in time to come. He no longer delayed selling his corn till he should meet the oil-merchant or the wool-dealer to offer them the thing they

35

wanted; he reckoned it enough to find money, being certain that for this he could always obtain any required commodity. The buyer, too, on his side, needed not to study what would suit the seller: money was always sure to satisfy all his demands. Before the invention of a circulating medium, a fortunate concurrence of conveniences was requisite for an exchange: whereas after this invention, there could scarcely be a buyer that did not find a seller, or a seller who did not find a buyer.

As exchanges, and afterwards sales and purchases, were voluntary, it might be inferred that all values were given for values completely equal. It is more correct, however, to say, that bargains were never made without advantages to both parties. The seller found a profit in selling, the buyer in buying. The one drew more advantages from the money which he received, than he would have done from his merchandise; the other more advantage from the merchandise which he acquired, than he would have done from his money. Both parties had gained, and hence the nation gained doubly by their bargain. On the same principle when a master set any workman to labour, and gave him in exchange for the work expected to be done, a wage which corresponded to the workman's maintenance during his labour; - both these contractors gained; the workman because he had received in advance the fruit of his labour before it was accomplished; - the master, because this workman's labour was worth more than his wages. The nation gained with both; for as the national wealth must, at the long run, be realized in enjoyment, Whatever augments the enjoyment of individuals, must be considered as a gain for all.

Thus the labour of man created wealth; but wealth, in its turn, created the labour of man. Wherever wealth offered a profit, a wage, a subsistence, it produced a class of men, eager to acquire them. The accumulation of primary labour had created the value of land, by unfolding its productive power. This power, as it seconded the labour, of man, henceforth became a species of wealth; and a person possessed of land might, without himself labouring, obtain payment for surrendering the use of it to such as laboured. Hence the origin of sales and leases of land. The farmer again might hire workmen to labour, and thus might acquire the advantages attached to exchanging present subsistence against distant produce. He incurred all the charges of cultivation, he drew all its profits, and left to his workmen nothing but their wages. Thus the revenues of land, all comprised in the annual crop, were divided among three classes of men, under the name of rent, profit, and wages; whilst a surplus included the seed and the farmer's advance.

The manufacturer again possessed machinery and materials: he offered to his labourers an immediate subsistence for the fruit of a labour which required time and long advances. He enabled them to live, he furnished them with lodging, tools, machinery, and paid himself with interest by their work. If, in his own hand, he had not enough of accumulated wealth, or enough of the money which represents it, to provide his workmen with all the advances which their enterprise required, and to wait for the sale of their labour, he borrowed money, and paid the lender an interest, analogous to the rent which a farmer pays his landlord. The labour of the workmen employed by him annually produced a certain quantity of goods, in the value of which were to be included the interest of capital for the money-lender, the rent of implements, machines, immovables, and all kinds of fixed capital; the profits of the head manufacturer, the wages of his workmen, and, lastly, the capital expended in raw materials, together with the whole of that capital which, as it circulates annually in the manufactory, must be deducted from its annual produce, in order to leave the net revenue.

The produce of the soil and of manufactories belonged often to climates very distant from those inhabited by their consumers. A class of men undertook to facilitate all kinds of exchange, on condition of sharing in the profits which it yields. These men gave money to the producer, at the time when his work was finished and ready for sale; after which having transported the merchandise to the place where it was wanted, they waited the consumer's convenience, and retailed to him in parcels what he could not purchase all at once. They did service to every one, and repaid themselves for it by the share which is named profits of trade. The advantage arising from a judicious management of exchanges was the origin of those profits. In the north, a producer reckoned two measures of his merchandize equivalent to one of southern merchandize. In the south, on the other hand, a producer reckoned two measures of his merchandize equivalent to one of northern merchandize. Between two equations so different there was room to cover all the expenses of transport, all the profits of trade, and interest for all the money advanced to carry it on. In fact, at the sale of such commodities transported by commerce, there must be realized, first the capital repaid to the manufacturer; then the wages of the sailors, carriers, clerks, and all persons employed by the trader; next the interest of all those funds to which he gives movement; and lastly, the mercantile profit.

Society requires something more than wealth; it would not be complete if it contained nothing but productive labourers. It requires administrators, judges, lawgivers; men employed about its general interests; soldiers and sailors to defend it. No one of those classes produces any thing; their labour never assumes a material shape; it is not susceptible of accumulation. Yet without their assistance all the wealth arising from productive labour would be destroyed by violence; and work would cease, if the labourer could not calculate on peaceably enjoying its fruits. To support this guardian population, a part must be deducted from the funds created annually by labour. But as the service done to the community, by such persons, how important soever it be, is felt by no one in particular; it cannot, like other services, be an object of exchange. The community itself was under the necessity of paying it by a forced contribution from the revenues of all. It was not long, indeed, till this contribution came to be regulated by the persons destined to profit from it; and hence the contributors were loaded without measure; civil and military offices were multiplied far beyond what the public weal required; there was too much government, too much defence of men, who were forced to accept those services, and to pay them, superfluous or even burdensome as they might be; and the rulers of nations, established to protect wealth, were often the main authors of its dilapidation.

Society needs that kind of labour which produces mental enjoyments; and as mental enjoyments are, nearly all, immaterial, the objects destined to satisfy them cannot be accumulated. Religion, science, the arts, yield happiness to man; their origin is labour, their end enjoyment; but what belongs only to the soul is not capable of being treasured up. If a nation, however, does not reckon literature and the arts among its wealth, it may reckon literary men and artists; the education they receive, the distinction they acquire, accumulate a high value on their heads; and the labour which they execute being often better paid than that of the most skilled workmen, may thus contribute to the spread of opulence.

Society, in the last place, needs those kinds of labour, the object of which is to take care of the persons, not the fortunes of men. Such labour may be of the most elevated, or of the most servile kind: according as it requires either the knowledge of nature and the command of her secrets, like the physician's labour, or merely complaisance and obedience to the will of a master, like the footman's labour. All of them are species of labour intended for enjoyment, and differing from productive labour, only in so far as their effects are incapable of accumulation. Hence, though they add to the well-being of a state, they do not add to its wealth; and such as are employed in them must live on voluntary contributions drawn from the revenue formed by other kinds of labour.

Chapter 3: Of Territorial Wealth

The riches proceeding from land should be the first to engage the attention of an economist or a legislator. They are the most necessary of all, because it is from the ground that our subsistence is derived; because they furnish the materials for every other kind of labour; and lastly, because, in preparation, they constantly employ the half, often much more than the half, of all the nation. The class of people who cultivate the ground are particularly valuable for bodily qualities fitted to make excellent soldiers, and for mental qualities fitted to make good citizens. The happiness of a rural population is also more easily provided for than that of a city population; the progress of this kind of wealth is more easily followed; and government is more culpable when it allows agriculture to decay, because it almost always lies in the power of government to make it flourish.

The annual revenue of land, or the annual crop, is decomposed, as we observed above, in the following manner. One part of the fruits, produced by labour, is destined to pay the proprietor for the assistance which the earth has given to the labour of men, and also for the interest of all the capital successively employed to improve the soil. This portion alone is called the net revenue. Another part of the fruits replaces what has been consumed in executing the labour to which the crop is due, the seed, and all the cultivator's advances. Economists call this portion the resumption. Another part remains for a profit to the person who directed the labours of the ground: it is proportionate to his industry and the capital advanced by him. Government likewise takes a share of all those fruits, and by various imposts diminishes the proprietor's rent, the cultivator's profit, and the day-labourer's wages, in order to form a revenue for another class of persons. Nor do the fruits distributed among the workmen, the superintendent of the labour, and the proprietor, entirely remain with them in kind: after having kept a portion requisite for their subsistence, the whole then equally part with what remains, in exchange for objects produced by the industry of towns; and it is by means of this exchange, that all other classes of the nation are supplied with food.

The net revenue of territorial produce is considered to be that portion which remains with proprietors after the expenses of cultivation have been paid. Proprietors frequently imagine that a system of cultivation is the better, the higher those rents are: what concerns the nation, however, what should engage the economist's undivided attention, is the gross produce, or the total amount of the crop; by which subsistence is provided for the whole nation, and the comfort of all classes is secured. The former comprehends but the revenue of the rich and idle; the latter farther comprehends the revenue of all such as labour, or cause their capital to labour.

But a gradual increase of the gross produce may itself be the consequence of a state of suffering, - if the population, growing too numerous, can no longer find a sufficient recompense in the wages of labour, and if, struggling without protection against the proprietors of land, to whom limitation of number gives all the advantage of a monopoly, that population is reduced to purchase, by excessive labour, so small an augmentation of produce, as to leave it constantly depressed by want, There is no department of political economy which ought not to be judged in its relation to the happiness of the people in general; and a system of social order is always bad when the greater part of the population suffers under it.

Commercial wealth is augmented and distributed by exchange; and even the produce of the ground, so soon as it is gathered in, belongs likewise to commerce. Territorial wealth, on the other hand, is created by means of permanent contacts. With regard to it, the economist's attention should first be directed to the progress of cultivation: next to the mode in which the produce of the harvest is distributed among those who contribute to its growth; and lastly, to the nature of those rights which belong to the proprietors of land, and to the effects

41

resulting from an alienation of their property.

The progress of social order, the additional security, the protection which government holds out to the rights of all, together with the increase of population, induce the cultivator to entrust to the ground, for a longer or shorter period, the labour which constitutes his wealth. In the timorous condition of barbarianism, he will not, at his own expense, increase the value of an immovable possession, which perhaps he may be forced to abandon at a moment's warning. But in the security of complete civilization, he regards his immovable possessions as more completely safe than any other kind of wealth. In the deserts of Arabia and Tartary; in the savannahs of America, before civilization has begun; in the pastures of the Campagna di Roma, or the Capitanata de la Pouille, after it has ended, men are contented with the natural fruits of the ground, with grass for their cattle to browse; and if those vast deserts yet retain any value, they owe it less to the slight labour by which the proprietor has inclosed them, than to the labour by which the herdsman has multiplied the oxen and sheep which feed upon them.

When the population of such deserts has begun to increase, and an agricultural life to succeed that of shepherds, men still abstain from committing to the ground any labour whose fruit they cannot gather till after many years have elapsed. The husbandman tills, to reap in the following season; the course of a twelvemonth is sufficient to give back all his advances. The earth which he has sown, far from gaining a durable value by his labour, is, for a time, impoverished by the fruits it has born. Instead of seeking to improve it by more judicious cultivation, he gives it back to the desert for repose, and next year tills another portion. The custom of fallowing, a remnant of this half savage mode of agriculture, continues to our own time, in more than three-fourths of Europe.

But when population and wealth have at last increased so as to make every kind of labour easy, and when social order

42

inspires security enough to induce the husbandman to fix his labour in the ground, and transmit it with the soil to his descendants, improvement altogether changes the appearance of the earth. Then are formed those plantations of gardens, orchards, vineyards, the enjoyment of which is destined for a late posterity; then are dug those canals for draining or irrigation, which diffuse fertility; then arise upon the hills those hanging terraces, which characterized the agriculture of ancient Canaan. A quick rotation of crops of a different nature reanimates, instead of exhausting, the strength of the soil; and a numerous population lives on a space, which, according to the primitive system, would hardly have supported a few scores of sheep.

The trade or the manufactures of a country, are not to be called prosperous, because a small number of merchants have amassed immense fortunes in it. On the contrary, their extraordinary profits almost always testify against the general prosperity of the country. So likewise, in counties abandoned to pasturage, the profits realized by some rich proprietors ought not to be regarded as indicating a judicious system of agriculture. Some individuals, it is true, grow rich; but the nation, which the land should maintain, or the food which should support it, are no where to be found. It is not even certain that the net produce of the land may not diminish, in proportion as its agriculture yields a more abundant produce, and a greater number of citizens live on its fruits; just as we see the net produce of money, or its interest, diminish in proportion as a country becomes more commercial, and contains more capital.

The first proprietors of land were doubtless themselves cultivators, and executed all kinds of field labour, with their children and servants. To these, in ancient times, were added slaves; the continual state of war, which exists among semi-barbarous societies, having introduced slavery at the remotest era. The stronger found it more convenient to procure workmen by the abuse of victory than by bargain. Yet so long as the head of each family laboured along with his children and slaves, the condition of the latter was less wretched; the master felt himself to be of the same nature with his servant; he experienced the same wants and the same fatigue; he desired the same pleasures, and knew, by experience, that he would obtain little work from a man whom he fed badly. Such was the patriarchal mode of cultivation, that of the golden days of Italy and Greece; such is that of free America; such appears to be that of Africa, in its interior; and such, finally, but without slavery, and therefore with still more domestic comfort, is that of Switzerland, where the peasant proprietor is happier than in any other country of the world.

Among the states of antiquity, the farms under cultivation were small; and the number of freemen labouring in the fields, always greatly surpassed that of slaves. The former had a full enjoyment of their persons and the fruits of their labour; the latter, degraded rather than unhappy, like the ox, man's companion, which interest teaches him to spare, seldom experienced suffering, want still more rarely. The head of each family alone receiving the total crop, did not distinguish the rent from the profit or the wages; with the excess of what he wanted for food, he procured the produce of the town in exchange, and this excess supported all other classes of the nation.

But the progress of wealth, of luxury, and idleness, in all the states of antiquity, substituted the servile for the patriarchal mode of cultivation. The population lost much in happiness and number by this change; the earth gained little in productiveness. The Roman proprietors extending their patrimonies by the confiscated territories of vanquished states; the Greeks by wealth acquired from trade, first abandoned manual labour, and soon afterwards, despised it. Fixing their residence in towns, they entrusted the management of their estates to stewards and inspectors of slaves; and from that period, the condition of most part of the country population became intolerable. Labour, which once been a point of communion betwixt the two ranks of society, now became a barrier of separation; contempt and

44

severity succeeded to affectionate care; punishments were multiplied as they came to be inflicted by inferiors, and as the death of one or several slaves did not lessen the steward's wealth. Slaves who were ill-fed, ill-teated, ill-recompensed, could not fail to lose all interest in their master's affairs, and almost all understanding. Far from attending to their business with affection, they felt a secret joy every time they saw their oppressors' wealth diminished, or his hopes deceived. The study of science, accompanied with habits of observation, certainly advanced the theory of agriculture: but its practice, at the same time, rapidly declined; a fact, which all the agricultural writers of antiquity lament. The cultivation of land was entirely divested of all that intelligence, affection, and zeal, which had once hastened its success. The revenues were smaller, the expenses greater; and from that period, it became an object to save labour, more than to augment its produce. Slaves, after having driven every free cultivator from the fields, were themselves rapidly decreasing in number. During the decline of the Roman empire, the population of Italy was not less reduced than that of the Agro Romano is in our days; while, at the same time, it had sunk into the that degree of wretchedness and penury. The cultivation of the colonies situated on the Mexican Gulf was founded, in like manner, on the baneful system of slavery. it has, in like manner, consumed the population, debased the human species, and deteriorated the system of agriculture. The negro trade has of course filled up those voids, which the barbarity of planters annually produced in the agricultural population; and doubtless, under a system of culture, such that the man who labours is constantly reduced below the necessaries of life, and the man who does not labour keeps all for himself, the net produce has always been considerable; but the gross produce, with which alone the nation is concerned, has uniformly been inferior to what would have arisen from any other system of cultivation, whilst the condition of more than seven-eighths of the population has continued to be miserable.

The invasions of the Roman empire, by the barbarians, introduced new manners, and, with them, new systems of cultivation. The conqueror, who had now become proprietor, being much less allured by the enjoyments of luxury, had need of men still more than of wealth. He had ceased to dwell in towns, he had established himself in the country; and his castle formed a little principality, which he wished to be able to defend by his own strength, and thus he felt the necessity of acquiring the affection of such as depended on him. A relaxation of the social bond, and the independence of great proprietors, produced the same effects without the limits of the ancient Roman empire as within. From the epoch of its downfall, masters in every part of Europe began to improve the condition of their dependents; and this return to humanity produced the natural effect; it rapidly increased the population, the wealth, and the happiness of rural labourers.

Different expedients were resorted to for giving slaves and cultivators an interest in life, a property, and an affection for the place of their nativity, as well as for its lord. Adopted by various states, these expedients produced the most decisive influence on territorial wealth and population. In Italy, and part of France and Spain, and probably in most part of the former Roman empire, the master shared the land among his vassals, and agreed with them to share the crops in a raw state. This is cultivation for half produce. In Hungary, Poland, Bohemia, and all that portion of Germany occupied by Slavonic tribes, the master much more rarely enfranchised his slaves. Keeping them always under an absolute dependence, as serfs attached to the soil, he gave them, however, one half of his land, reserving the other to himself. He wished to share, not the fruits of their labour, but their labour itself, and therefore he obliged them to work for him two, three, and in Transylvania, four days of each week. This is cultivation by corvees. In Russia, and several provinces of France and England, masters likewise distributed their lands among vassals; but, instead of wishing to participate either in the lands or the harvests, they imposed a fixed capitation. Such was the abundance of uncultivated land always ready to be cleared, that, in the eyes of those proprietors, the only difference in the condition of agricultural families was the number of workmen included in them. To capitation was always joined the obligation of personal service, and the vassal's continuance in a servile state. Yet, according as the laws watched more or less strictly over the subject's liberty, cultivation upon this principle raised the husbandman to a condition more or less comfortable. In Russia, he never escaped from servitude of the soil; in England, by an easy transition, he arrived at the rank of farmer.

The system of cultivation by metayers, or cultivation at half produce, is perhaps one of the best inventions of the middle ages. It contributes, more than any thing else, to diffuse happiness among the lower classes, to raise land to a high state of culture, and accumulate a great quantity of wealth upon it. It is the most natural, the easiest, and most advantageous step for exalting the slave to the condition of a freeman, for opening his understanding, teaching him economy and temperance, and placing in his hands a property which he will not abuse. According to this system, the peasant is supposed to have no capital, or scarcely any, but he receives the land sown and fully stocked; he takes the charge of continuing every operation, of keeping his farm in the same state of culture, of delivering to his master the half of each crop; and, when the lease expires, of returning the land under seed, the folds furnished, the vines propped, and every thing, in short, in the same state of completeness as it was when he received it.

A metayer finds himself delivered from all those cares which, in other counties, weigh heavily on the lower class of the people. He pays no direct tax, his master alone is charged with it; he pays no money-rent, and therefore he is not called to sell or to buy, except for his own domestic purposes. The term, at which the farmer has to pay his taxes or his rent, does not press the metayer; or constrain him to sell before the season, at a low price, the crop which rewards his industry. He needs but little capital, because he is not a dealer in produce; the fundamental advances have been made once for all by his master; and as to the daily labour, he performs it himself with his family; for cultivation upon this principle brings constantly along with it a great division of the land, or what is called cultivation on the small scale.

Under this system, the peasant has an interest in the property, as if it were his own; without the anxieties of wealth, he finds in his farm every enjoyment, with which nature's liberality rewards the labour of man. His industry, his economy, the development of his understanding, regularly increase his little stock. In good years, he enjoys a kind of opulence; he is not entirely excluded from the feast of nature which he prepares; his labour is directed according to the dictates of his own prudence, and the plants that his children may gather the fruit. The high state of culture to be found in the finest parts of Italy, above all of Tuscany, where the lands are generally managed in this way. the accumulation of an immense capital upon the soil: the invention of many judicious rotations, and industrious processes, which an intelligent, observing spirit alone could have deduced from the operations of nature; the collection of a numerous population, upon a space very limited and naturally barren, shows plainly enough that this mode of cultivation is as profitable to the land itself as to the peasant, and that, if it imparts most happiness to the lower class who live by the labour of their hands, it also draws from the ground the most abundant produce, and scatters it with most profusion among men.

But whenever a country arrives at complete civilization, whenever the property and safety of individuals are sufficiently protected, the usual population increases beyond what husbandry can employ; the extent of land is limited, the population is not so. A great number of families are brought up on one farm, and sent away by some accidental cause; penury compels them to offer their services to some proprietor, for a recompence smaller than what is given to such as are actually employed. Labourers outbid each other, and at length go so far as to content themselves with the most niggardly subsistence, with a portion barely sufficient in good years, and which in bad years leaves them a prey to famine. This foolish species of competition has reduced the peasantry on the coast of Genoa, in the republic of Lucca, in several provinces of the kingdom of Naples, to content themselves with a third of the crop, in place of a half. In a magnificent country, which nature has enriched with all her gifts; which art has adorned with all its luxury; which annually gives forth a most abundant harvest - the numerous class that produce the fruits of the ground never taste the corn which is reaped or the wine which is pressed, by their labour, and struggle continually with famine. The same misfortune would probably have happened to the people of Tuscany, if public opinion had not guarded the farmer; but there no proprietor dares to impose terms unusual in the country, and when he changes one metayer for another, he changes no article of the primitive contact. So soon, however, as public opinion becomes necessary for the maintenance of public prosperity, it ought, in strict propriety, to be sanctioned by law. Whenever vacant lands are no longer to be found, proprietors of the soil come to exercise a kind of monopoly against the rest of the nation; and wherever monopoly exists, the legislature ought to interpose, lest they who enjoy may also abuse it.

Cultivation by corvees was very far from being as happy an invention. No doubt it gave to the peasantry a kind of property, an interest in life; but it reduced them to see their domestic economy disturbed every moment, by the vexatious demands of a landlord or his stewards. The peasant could not perform the operations of his husbandry at the day fixed upon; the landlord's work must always be done before his own; the rainy days constantly fell to the share of the weaker party. Under this system, the labourer performs every service for his master with repugnance, without care for its success, without affection, and without reward. In the landlord's fields, he works as badly as he can without incurring punishment. The steward, on the other hand, declares it absolutely necessary that corporal penalties be employed; and the infliction of them is abandoned to his own discretion. Servitude of the soil has nominally been abolished in several countries, which have adopted the system of cultivation by corvees; but so long as this general system of agriculture is in force, there cannot be any liberty for the peasant. And although the abolition of servitude has given vassals a property and right, which the landlord did not formerly acknowledge, it has hardly at all bettered their conditions. They are as constantly thwarted and disturbed in their own operations as before; they work quite as ill during the landlord's day's; they are quite as miserable within their huts; and the master, who had been flattered with hopes that the abolition of slavery would increase his revenue, has derived no advantage from it. On the contrary, he is ever an object of hatred and distrust to his vassals; and social order, threatened so incessantly, cannot be maintained except by violent means.

The ground of the metayer's contract is every way the same, as that of a contract with the cultivator by corvees. The landlord in Hungary, as in Italy. has given up his land to the peasant, on condition of receiving half its fruits in return. In both countries, the other half has been reckoned sufficient for supporting the cultivator, and repaying his advances. A single error in political economy has rendered what is highly advantageous for one of these countries disastrous for the other. The Hungarian has not inspired the labourer with any interest in his own industry. by sharing the land and the days of the week, he has made an enemy of the man, who should have been his coadjutor. The labour is performed without zeal or intelligence; the master's share, inferior to what it would have been according to the other system, is collected with fear; the peasant's share is so reduced, that he lives in constant penury; and some of the most fertile counties in the world have already been for ages doomed to this state of wretchedness and oppression.

But the legislator's interference, which we claimed for

the metayer, has, in some of the countries cultivated by corvees, actually taken place in favour of the vassal, peasant, or serf. In the German provinces of the Austrian monarchy, contracts between the landlord and peasant are, by law, made irrevocable, and most of the corvees have been changed into a fixed and perpetual rent of money, or of fruits in a raw state. By this means, the peasant has acquired a true property in his house and land: only, it continues to be charged with rents, and some feudal services. Still farther to protect the peasantry from being afterwards oppressed or gradually expelled from their properties, by the opulent lords living among them, the law does not allow any noble to buy a vassal's land; or, if he does buy any, he is obliged to sell it, on the same conditions, to some other family of peasants; so that the property of the nobles can never increase, or the agricultural population diminish.

These regulations of the Austrian government in behalf of an order, which, if left to itself, must needs be oppressed, are almost sufficient to redeem the errors of its general system, by this increase of happiness to the subject, and of stability to the system itself. In a country deprived of liberty, where the finances have at all times been wretchedly administered, where wars are eternal - and still disastrous, obstinacy there being always joined with incapacity; the great mass of the population, composed almost wholly of peasant-proprietors living in easy circumstances, have been rendered happy; and this mass of subjects, feeling their own happiness, and dreading every change, have mocked all the projects of revolution or of conquest directed against their country, the government of which is so little able to defend itself.

The system of cultivating land by capitation, could be adopted only among a people scarcely emerged from barbarism. It is, in fact, nearly a modern farm-lease, the parties to which, in fixing the rent, pay no regard to the greater or smaller extent of the ground, to its comparative fertility or barrenness, to the improvements which labour has already made it undergo. Be the nature of those circumstances what it may, each proprietor of a whole Russian province pays thirty roubles yearly to the lord of it. Doubtless when the capitation was imposed, all those circumstances were equal; there was more fertile land for each than each could cultivate, and no part of it had yet been improved by labour.

In free counties, capitation is looked upon as a degrading tax, because it recalls the idea of servitude. It was, indeed, originally always accompanied with servitude of the soil. The peasant always depended on the good pleasure of his master; in executing their mutual contact, no law afforded him protection; he was always liable to be ejected, carried off, sold, stript of all the property amassed by his industry; and thus the kind of authority to which he was subject incessantly reminded him, that, whatever he saved, he took from himself to give it to his master; that every effort on his part was useless, every invention dangerous, every improvement contrary to his interest, and finally, that every sort of study but aggravated his wretchedness by more clearly informing him of his condition.

Even in Russia, however, the disinterestedness of some noble families, who for several generations have not changed the capitation, has inspired the peasantry with confidence sufficient to reanimate their industry, to infuse a taste for labour and economy, and sometimes even to permit their realizing very large fortunes which, however, always depend on the master's good pleasure. But in countries where servitude of the soil has been gradually abolished, the capitation has become a fixed rent; united most frequently to personal services, and sometimes reduced to mere feudal rights, as the system, by degrees, varied from its primitive uniformity. Such was the tenure by villanage in France, by copy-hold in England, the origin of nearly all the property possessed by peasants cultivating their own heritages. On the other hand, such contracts helped to produce the notion of farm-leases, which, in the wealthiest countries of Europe, have succeeded every other kind of convention between proprietor and cultivator.

By a farm-lease, the proprietor yields his land, and nothing more, to the cultivator; and demands an invariable rent for it; whilst the farmer undertakes to direct and to execute all the labour by himself; to furnish the cattle, the implements, and the funds of agriculture; to sell his produce, and to pay his taxes. The farmer takes upon him all the cares and all the gains of his agriculture; he teats it as a commercial speculation, from which he expects a profit proportionate to the capital employed in it.

At the time when slavery was abolished, the system of farms could not be immediately established: freedmen could not yet undertake such important engagements, nor were they able to advance the labour of a year, much less that of several years, for putting the farm in a proper condition. The master, on giving them their liberty, would have been obliged to give them also an establishment; to furnish them with cattle, instruments of tillage, seed and food for a year; and after all these advances, the farm would still have been a burdensome concern for the owner, because by his contract he had renounced the profit of good years on condition that his farmer should warrant him against bad years; but the farmer who had nothing could warrant nothing, and the master would have given up his good crops without any return.

The first farmers were mere labourers; they executed most of the agricultural operations with their own hands; they adjusted their enterprises to the strength of their families; and as the proprietor reposed little confidence in their management, he used to regulate their procedure by numerous obligatory clauses; he limited their leases to a few years, and kept them in a continual state of dependence. During the last century, farmers, particularly in England, have risen to rank and importance. Political writers and legislators have uniformly viewed them with a favourable eye; their leases have ceased to be limited in time to a small number of years, and hence farmers have issued from a more elevated class of society. With large capitals, they have taken farms of a larger size; more extensive knowledge, and a better education have enabled them to teat agriculture as a science: They have applied to it several important discoveries in chemistry and natural history; they have also in some degree united the habits of the merchant with those of the cultivator. The hope of a larger profit has induced them to make larger advances; they have renounced that parsimony which originates in want, and stands in direct opposition to enlightened economy; they have calculated and recorded the result of their operations with greater regularity, and this practice has furnished better opportunities of profiting by their own experience.

On the other hand, farmers from this time have ceased to be labourers; and below them has of course been formed a class of men of toil, who, being entrusted with supporting the whole nation by their labour, are the real peasants, the truly essential part of the population. The peasantry, strengthened by the kind of labour most natural to man, are perpetually required for recruiting all the other classes; it is they who must defend the country in a case of need; whom it most concerns us to attach to the soil where they were born; and policy itself would invite every government to render their lot happy, even though humanity did not command it.

When the system of small farms has been compared, as is often done, with that of great farms, it has not been sufficiently considered that the latter, by taking the direction of his labour out of the peasant's hands, reduces him to a condition greatly more unhappy than almost any other system of cultivation. In truth, hinds performing all the labours of agriculture, under the command of a rich farmer, are not only more dependent than metayers, but even than serfs, who pay their capitation or their service. The latter, whatever vexations they experience, have at least a hope, a property, and a heritage to leave their children. But the hind has no participation in property, nothing to hope from the fertility of the toil or the propitiousness of the season; he plants not for his children; he entrusts not to the ground the labour of his young years, to reap the fruit of it, with interest, in his old age. He lives each week on the wages of the last. Ever exposed to the want of work by derangements in his master's fortune; ever ready to feel the extremes of want, from sickness, accident, or even the approaches of old age, he runs all the risks of ruin without enjoying any of the chances of fortune. Economy in his situation is scarcely probable; but though he should succeed in collecting a little capital, the suppression of all intermediate ranks hinders him from putting it to use. The distance between his lot and that of an extensive farmer, is too great for being passed over; whereas, in the system of cultivation on the small scale, a labourer may succeed, by his little economy, in acquiring a small farm or a small metairie; from this he may pass to a greater, and from that to every thing. The same causes have suppressed all the intermediate stages in other departments of industry. A gulf lies between the day-labourer and every enterprise of manufacture or trade, as well as farming; and the lower classes have now lost that help which sustained them in a former period of civilization. Parish aids, which are secured to the day-labourer, increase his dependence. In such a state of suffering and disquietude, it is not easy to preserve the feeling of human dignity, or the love of freedom; and thus at the highest point of modern civilization, the system of agriculture approximates to that of those corrupt periods of ancient civilization, when the whole labour of the field was performed by slaves.

The state of Ireland, and the convulsions to which that unhappy country is continually exposed, show clearly enough how important it is for the repose and security of the rich themselves, that the agricultural class, which forms the great majority of a nation, should enjoy conveniences, hope, and happiness. The Irish peasants are ready to revolt, and plunge their country into the horrors of civil war; they live each in a miserable hut, on the produce of a few beds of potatoes, and the milk of a cow; more unhappy, at the present day, than the cottagers of England, though possessing a small property, of which the latter are destitute. In return for their allotted portion of ground, they merely engage to work by the day, at a fixed wage, on the farm where they live; but their competition with each other has forced them to be satisfied with a wage of the lowest possible kind. A similar competition will act likewise against the English cottagers. There is no equality of strength between the day-labourer, who is starving, and the farmer, who does not even lose the revenue of his ground, by suppressing some of his habitual operations; and hence the result of such a struggle between the two classes, is constantly a sacrifice of the class which is poorer, more numerous, and better entitled to the protection of law.

Rich proprietors generally find that for themselves large farms are more advantageous than small ones. The small farmer rarely employs a capital sufficient even for his little cultivation; himself is always so near to ruin, that he must begin by ruining the ground. And certainly, in counties where the different systems of cultivation are practically set in opposition to each other, it is granted that land is ruined by letting it on lease, and reimproved by cultivating it with servants or metayers. It is not, therefore, small farms, but metairies, which ought to be compared with large farms. Cultivation on the great scale, spares much time which is lost in the other way; it causes a greater mass of work to be performed in the same time, by a given number of men; it tends, above all, to procure from the employment of great capitals the profit formerly procured from the employment of numerous workmen; it introduces the use of expensive instruments, which abridge and facilitate the labour of man. It invents machines, in which the wind, the fall of water, the expansion of steam, are substituted for the power of limbs; it makes animals execute the work formerly executed by men. It hunts the latter from trade to trade, and concludes by rendering their existence useless. Any saving of human strength is a prodigious advantage, in a colony, where the supernumerary population may always be advantageously employed. Humanity justly solicits the employment of machines to aid the labour of the negroes, who cannot perform what is required of them, and who used to be incessantly recruited by an infamous commerce. But in a country where population is already too abundant, the dismissal of more than half the field-labourers is a serious misfortune, particularly at a time when a similar improvement in machinery causes the dismissal of more than half the manufacturing population of towns. The nation is nothing else but the union of all the individuals who compose it, and the progress of its wealth is illusory, when obtained at the price of general wretchedness and morality.

Whilst, in England, the peasantry are hastening to destruction, their condition is improving in France; they are gathering strength, and without abandoning manual labour, they enjoy a kind of affluence; they unfold their minds, and adopt, though slowly, the discoveries of science. But in France, the peasants are mostly proprietors: the number of those who cultivate their own lands prodigiously increased in the revolution; and to this cause must be attributed the rapid progress which agriculture is making in that country, in spite of a long war and heavy contributions. Perhaps England might partly obtain a similar advantage, if these vast commons were shared among her cottagers, to whom the charm of property would thus be restored.

The most industrious provinces of France are, at this time, experiencing the unlooked - for effects of dividing property among its true cultivators; we mean the distribution of great farms among the contiguous peasantry, by a great number or particular contacts. A large proprietor now rarely gives his farm to be cultivated by a single person; he finds it infinitely more advantageous, at present, to share his domain among a number of neighbouring peasants, each of whom takes as much land as is requisite to occupy him all the year. No doubt, the peasant will generally sacrifice the land which he farms, to that which is his property; but both those portions are cultivated with the ardour which a direct interest excites in the labourer and with the intelligence which is developed in him, now that his lord can no longer oppress him. The agricultural classes are as happy as the political circumstances of a country, loved with enthusiasm, permit them to be.

To conclude our review of the systems, by which territorial wealth is incessantly renewed, we ought yet to bestow a moment of attention on the system of emphyteuses or perpetual farms, the most suitable of all when government has grants of land to make.

In other systems of cultivation, the agriculturist acquires all the fruit of his annual advances, but he can never be sure of profiting from those irredeemable advances by which a perpetual value is added to land, from drainings, plantations, and breaking up of the soil. Proprietors, of themselves, are seldom enabled to make such advances. If they sell the land, the purchaser, in order to acquire it, must surrender that very capital, with which he might have made those improvements. The lease of emphyteusis or plantation, which is the proper meaning of the word, was thus a very useful invention, as by it the cultivator engaged to break up a desert, on condition of acquiring the dominium utile of it for ever, whilst the proprietor reserved for himself an invariable rent to represent the dominium directum. No expedient could more happily combine, in the same individual, affection for property, with zeal for cultivation; or more usefully employ, in improving land, the capital destined to break it up. Although this kind of lease is known in England under the name of freehold for many lives; and though it is even of great importance in this kingdom, as the right of voting in county elections depends upon it, its beneficial influence has chiefly been experienced in Italy, where it is named livello. In the latter country, it has restored to the most brilliant state of cultivation whole provinces, which had been allowed to run waste. It cannot, however, become a universal mode of cultivation, because it deprives the direct proprietor of all the enjoyment of property, exposing him to all the inconveniences, with none of the advantages, in the condition of the capitalist; and because the father of a family can never be looked upon as prudent or economical, when he thus alienates his property for ever, without at least retaining the disposal of the price to be received in exchange for it.

For re-producing territorial wealth, it is sufficient, in general, that the use of the ground be transmitted to the industrious man, who may turn it to advantage, whilst the property of it continues with the rich man, who has no longer the same incitements or the same fitness for labour, and who thinks only of enjoyment. The national interest, however. sometimes also requires that property itself shall pass into hands likely to make a better use of it. It is not for themselves alone that the rich elicit the fruits of the earth; it is for the whole nation; and if, by a derangement in their fortune, they suspend the productive power of the country, it concerns the whole nation to put their property under different managers. Personal interest is, indeed, sufficient to bring about this transmission, provided the law offers no obstacle. When a soldier comes to inherit a machine for making stockings, he does not keep it long; in his hands, the machine is useless for himself and the nation; in the hands of a stocking-maker it would be productive, both for the nation and the individual. Both feel this; and a bargain is soon struck. The soldier receives money, which he well knows how to employ; the stocking-maker receives possession of his frame, and production recommences. Most of our European laws respecting immovable property, are like a law made to hinder the soldier from parting with the frame, of whose use he is ignorant.

The value of land cannot be unfolded, except by employing a capital sufficient to procure the accumulation of that labour which improves it. Hence, it is essential to the very existence of a nation that its land be always in the hands of those who can devote capital to its cultivation. If it were not in any case allowed to sell a workman's implement, it would not, certainly, at least, be forbidden to make new ones for the use of new workmen; but new lands cannot be made, and so often as the law prevents the alienation of an estate by one that cannot use it, so often does it suspend the most essential of all productions.

The systems of cultivation, which we have now glanced over in review, certainly cause the earth to produce, by the hands of temporary cultivators, when the permanent advances have been made; but they absolutely discourage such cultivators from making those permanent advances which, as they give a perpetual value to property, cannot be laid out except by those with whom that property is destined to continue. Legislators in general, altogether occupied with preventing the alienation of immovables, and preserving great fortunes in great families, have dreaded lest such an alienation might clandestinely be brought about by a lease, for a long term, and without return. They have eagerly attempted to defend the rights of proprietors against proprietors themselves; they have guided that class of people by forfeits and resolutory clauses; they have fixed upon a short term for farm leases; they seem continually repeating to the cultivator: "This land, on which you work, is not yours; acquire not too much affection for it; make no advances which you might run the risk of losing; improve the present moment, if you can, but think not of the future; above all, beware of labouring for posterity."

Besides, independently of legislative errors, it belongs to the very nature of a farm lease never to allow the farmer to take as much interest in the land as its proprietor. It is enough that this lease must have an end, to induce the farmer, as this end approaches, to care less about his fields, and to cease laying out money for improving them. The metayer, with smaller power, at least never fears to improve the land committed to him as much as possible; because the conditions of his lease are invariable, and he is never dismissed except for bad behaviour. The farmer, again, is liable to be dismissed directly in consequence of his good management. The more he has improved his farm, the more will his landlord, at renewing the lease, be disposed to require an augmentation of rent; and, besides, as part nf the advances laid out by the cultivator, on the ground, create a

60

perpetual value, it is neither just nor natural that they should be made by one whose interest is merely temporary. The farmer will carefully attend to the fields and meadows, which, in a few years, are to give him back all his advances; but he will plant few orchards; few high forests in the north; few vineyards in the south; he will make few canals for navigation, irrigation, or draining; he will transport little soil from one place to another; he will clear little ground; he will execute, in short, few of those works which are most conducive to the public interest, because they found the wealth of posterity.

None of those labours, on which the increase of the whole national subsistence depends, can be undertaken, save by a proprietor, rich in movable capital. It is not the preservation of great fortunes that concerns the nation, but the union of territorial fortunes with circulating ones. The fields do not flourish in the hands of those who have already too much wealth to watch over them, but in the hands of those who have enough of money to bring them into value. Territorial legislation ought, therefore, without ceasing, to strive that movable capital be united with fixed; property which we call personal with property which we call real. Legislation, over almost all the world, has striven to do quite the contrary.

And first, it were always for the national advantage, and favourable to the increase of its production, that the proprietor, whenever his fortune is embarrassed, should sell his property, instead of borrowing on it; yet, on the contrary, facilities have been held out to him for borrowing, rather than for sale. A particular system of law has been created for territorial debts; marked differences have been established between real and personal property; the rank of creditors on land has been regulated according to their date, whilst an absolute equality prevails among creditors of all dates, who claim only on movable property. And thus thousands of law-suits have been created, interminable difficulties have been started, and the time is almost come when half the lands of Europe are possessed by a people who far from possessing the power to dispose of a capital that might increase their productiveness, on the contrary, are debtors by a pretty large capital, which they cannot extract from those funds. Hence those embarrassed proprietors have incessantly had recourse to ruinous expedients not to put money on their lands, but to take it off; to borrow of their farmers, to diminish the funds of cultivation, to sell their woods, and deteriorate their estates. If the law had given no preference to territorial creditors; if, on the other hand it had given as much facility to a creditor for selling an immovable property, as for making seizure of a movable one; especially, if, in protecting personal liberty, sacrificed too slightly, it had permitted lands to be sold as often as it now permits the debtor to be put in prison - most old debts would be extinguished, and those immovable possessions, which ought to support the nation, would be in the hands of such as could force them, by capital and labour, to furnish the means of subsistence.

But the props lent to the pride of family by entails, fideicommissa, primogenitures, and the laws invented to hinder families in a ruinous condition from selling their property, have still further impeded the development of agriculture and industry. The legislator aimed at fixing fortune in great families: he has fixed beggary and want in them. On pretext of securing the patrimony of children, he has forbidden the heir of entail to sell or borrow with a sufficient security to his creditors; but he could not hinder him from going to ruin, and overwhelming himself with clamorous debts. In that case, even the care of his honour, the feeling of justice, and his own security, oblige him to employ all the resources of his mind, all his industry in destroying his patrimony, that he may obtain the disposal of what law has reserved to his heir. Whatever produce he can detach from the ground without replacing it, whatever advance he can dispense with laying out, is, in his eyes, just so much profit; and Europe has come to see the proprietors of noble estates, almost everywhere, the enemies of their property. At the same time, if the legislator's object was the preservation of families, he has failed in this object; because entails condemn all the sons of a rich family to idleness; the elder out of pride, the younger out of inability. The system has proscribed all from industry, the sole mean of increasing property; whilst it leaves them subject to all human chances, which never cease to attack whatever is ancient, and which must always, in the end, destroy whatever opulence is not renewed.

Chapter 4: Of Commercial Wealth

By labour man drew his first wealth from the earth, but scarcely had he satisfied his primitive wants, when desire made him conceive other enjoyments, not to be obtained without the aid of his fellows. Exchanges began. They extended to whatever had any value, to whatever could produce any; they comprised mutual services and labour, no less than the fruit of labour; and gave room to the formation and increase of a new kind of wealth, which was no longer measured by the wants of him who produced it, but by the wants of all those with whom he might transact exchanges, - with whom he might carry on commerce; and hence we have named it commercial wealth.

The solitary man was used to labour for his own wants, and his consumption was the measure of his production; he fitted out a place to produce him provisions for a year, for two years perhaps; but afterwards he did not indefinitely augment it. It was enough to renew the process, so as to maintain himself in the same condition; and, if he had time to spare, he laboured at acquiring some new enjoyment, at satisfying some other fancy. Society has never done any thing by commerce, except sharing among all its members what the isolated man would have prepared solely for himself. Each labours, in like manner, to provide for all, during a year, two years, or more; each labours, afterwards, to keep up this provision, according as consumption destroys a part of it; and since the division of labour and the improvement of arts allow more and more work to be done, each, perceiving that he has already provided for the reproduction of what has been consumed, studies to awaken new tastes and new fancies which he may satisfy.

But when a man laboured for himself alone, he never dreamt of those fancies, till he had provided for his wants; his time was his revenue; his time formed also his whole means of production. There was no room to fear, that the one would not be exactly proportioned to the other; that he would ever work to satisfy an inclination that he did not feel, or which he valued less than a want. But when trade was introduced, and each no longer laboured for himself, but for an unknown person, the different proportions subsisting between the desire and what could satisfy it, between the labour and the revenue, between production and consumption, were no longer equally certain; they were independent of each other, and every workman was obliged to regulate his conduct by guessing on a subject, concerning which the most skilful had nothing but conjectural information.

The isolated man's knowledge of his own means and his own wants, required to be replaced by a knowledge of the market, for which the social man was labouring; of its demands and its extent.

The number of consumers, their tastes, the extent of their consumption, and their income, regulate the market for which every producer labours. Each of these four elements is variable, independently of the rest, and each of their variations accelerates or retards the sale. The number of consumers may decrease, not only by sickness or war, but also by obstacles which policy may place in the way of their communication, or by the avarice of new sellers. Their tastes may be changed by fashion: an extraordinary consumption of one kind of merchandize, brought about by some public calamity, may have reduced them to be frugal in all the rest; and finally, their income may diminish without a diminution of their number, and with the same wants, the same means of satisfying them may no longer exist. Such revolutions in the market are difficult to know with precision, difficult to calculate; and their obscurity is greater for each individual producer, because he but imperfectly knows the number and means of his rivals, the merchants, who are to sell in competition with him. But one single observation serves him, instead of all them: he compares his price with that of the buyer, and this comparison, according to the profit or loss which it offers him, is a warning to increase or diminish his production, for the following year.

The producer establishes his price according to what the merchandise has cost, including his profit, which ought to be proportional to what might be obtained in any other kind of industry. The price must be sufficient to repay the workmen's wages, the rent of the land, or the interest on the fixed capitals employed in production, the raw materials wrought by him, with all the expenses of transport, and all the advances of money. When all these reimbursements, calculated at the mean rate of the country, are themselves repaid by the last purchaser, the production may continue on the same footing. If the profits rise above the mean rate, the producer will extend his enterprizes; he will employ new hands and fresh capital, and, striving to benefit by this extraordinary profit, he will soon reduce it to the common level. If the buyer, on the other hand, pays a price too low for compensating all the producer's reimbursements, the latter will, of course, seek to reduce his production, but this change will not be so easy as the other. The workmen employed by him, rather than abandon what gains their bread, consent to work at a lower price; for less even than the necessaries of life. Fixed capitals, moreover, cannot be put to another use; he will content himself with a smaller profit, and continue to work with them till they produce next to nothing. Lastly, the manufacturer himself must live by his industry, and never willingly abandons it: he is ever disposed to attribute the decline of his last year's trade to accidental causes; and the less he has gained, the less is he willing to retire from business. Thus production continues almost always longer than demand, unless the manufacturer has, of his own accord, renounced his business to attempt a new one.

The buyer's price, an the other hand, is fixed by competition. He does not inquire what the article costs, but what are the terms on which he may obtain another to serve in its stead; he addresses himself to various merchants, who offer him the same commodity, and bargains with him who will sell the cheapest; or else he considers which will suit him best, among several articles of a different nature, but capable of being substituted for each other. As each is occupied solely with his own private interest, each tends to the same object: all the buyers, on one hand, all the sellers on the other, act as if in concert: the sums asked, and the sums offered, are brought to an equilibrium, and the mean price is established.

The seller's price should enable him to reproduce the article sold, with a profit, under the same condition, in the same place. His market, therefore, extends to every country where the mean price established by commerce is no smaller than his. His production is not limited by the consumption of neighbors or countrymen; it is regulated by the whole number of those who, whatever country they inhabit, find an advantage in purchasing his goods, or for whom his producing price is not superior to the buying price. It is this which properly constitutes the extent of market.

As the division of labour incessantly augments its productive powers, and the increase of capitals daily obliges the merchant to seek new employment for industry, and try new manufactures, the producer feels no interest more pressing than that of extending his market. If he cannot find new places of sale, it will neither suit him to enlarge his manufactory, when his capital has been increased by saving, nor to improve his fabrication by performing more work with the same machinery, or the same number of hands. The whole progress of his fortune depends on the progress of his sale.*

Among the causes which augment this sale, the first is the discovery of such an economy in labour as may enable the manufacturer to sell cheaper than his brethren, and to get possession of their custom: he will sell more, but they will sell less. The consumers will make a light saving; yet, if both are subjects of the same state, the difference in regard to the national interest will not be great. The distress of those producers, who have lost their custom, and who, probably, will lose a considerable part of their capital by selling their wares too cheap, and abandoning their former machinery, will perhaps counterbalance the profit of purchasers.

As policy is wont to comprise the obligation of social duties within the circle of our countrymen, the mutual rivalship of foreign producers has more openly displayed itself. They have striven to exclude each other from the markets, where they came in competition, by selling at a cheaper rate. Every national discovery, which allows the producers of one country to sell cheaper than those of other countries, inevitably increases the former's production at the latter's expense; and the profit of this saving is shared between producers who extend their market, and consumers who provide for their wants at a smaller expense. Yet if a single manufacturer has succeeded in making this saving, which extends his market; or if the exclusive use of it is secured to him by patent, his countrymen. also manufacturers, against whom he has made this successful competition, must support all the loss of it, whilst himself and the foreign consumer share all the profit. In an age, when communication among different counties is easy, when all the sciences are applied to all the arts, discoveries are soon divined and copied, and a nation cannot long retain an advantage in manufacturing which it owes but to a secret; so that the market, extended for a moment by a fall in the price, is very soon shut up; and if the general consumption is not increased, the production is not so either.

Sale is extended also, and in a more lasting manner, when the cheapness of the thing produced brings it within the reach of a new class of consumers; a very sensible diminution of the price may often produce this effect. Thus glass windows were at one time confined to palaces; they are found at the present time in the meanest huts. Consumption is in that case truly increased; each nation gains doubly by it; manufacturers have extended their labour; the poor have acquired a new enjoyment.

The increase of population, and of national wealth, contributes to extend the market, in a manner still more advantageous. Yet every conceivable increase of population and of wealth, does not, of necessity, extend the market; it is only such an increase as attends the increased comforts of the most numerous class. When cultivation on the great scale has succeeded cultivation on the small, more capital is perhaps absorbed by land, and re-produced by it; more wealth than formerly may be diffused among the whole mass of agriculturists, but the consumption of one rich farmer's family, united to that of fifty families of miserable hinds, is not so valuable for the nation, as that of fifty families of peasants, no one of which was rich, but none deprived of an honest competence. So also in towns, the consumption of a manufacturer worth a million, under whose orders are employed a thousand workmen, reduced to the bare necessaries of life, is not so advantageous for the nation, as that of a hundred manufacturers far less rich, who employ each but ten workmen far less poor. It is very true, that ten thousand pounds of income, whether they belong to a single man, or to a hundred, are all equally destined for consumption, but this consumption is not of the same nature. A man, however rich, cannot employ for his use an infinitely greater number of articles than a poor man, but he employs articles infinitely better; he requires work far better finished, materials far more precious, and brought from a far greater distance. It is he who especially encourages the perfection of certain workmen, that finish a small number of objects with extreme skill; it is he who pays them an exorbitant wage. It is he also that especially rewards such workmen as we have named unproductive, because they procure for him nothing but fugitive enjoyments, which can never by accumulation form part of the national wealth; and whilst the effect of increasing capital is generally to concentrate labour in very large manufactories, the effect of great opulence is almost entirely to exclude the produce of those large manufactories from the consumption of the opulent man. The diffusion of wealth, therefore, still more than its accumulation, truly constitutes national prosperity, because it keeps up the kind of consumption most favourable for national re-production.

The manufacturer's market may, in the last place, be extended, by what forms the noblest wish of a statesman, the progress of civilization, comfort, security, and happiness, among barbarous nations. Europe has arrived at such a point, that, in all its parts, there is to be found an industry, a quantity of fabrication, superior to its wants; but if false policy did not incessantly induce us to arrest the progress of civilization among our neighbours; if Egypt had been left in the hands of a people requiring the arts of Europe; if Turkey were extricated from the oppression under which it groans; if our victories over the inhabitants of Barbary had been profitably employed in giving back the coasts of Africa to social life; if Spain had not again been yielded to a despotism which destroys and ruins her population; if the independents of America were protected, so that they might be allowed to enjoy the advantages which nature offers them; if the Hindoos, subject to Europe, were amalgamated with Europeans; if Franks were encouraged to settle among them, in place of being repelled, - consumption would increase in these different counties, rapidly enough to employ all this super-abundant labour, which Europe at present knows not how to dispose of, and to terminate this distress in which the poor are plunged.

The more superior the buyer's price is to the seller's, the more profit does trade give to be shared among the trader, and all those whom he employs in the transport and distribution of his goods; the manufacturer, and all those whom he employs in the production of them. Hence one of the great and constant objects of governments has been, to increase this difference, that their manufacturers might be enabled to produce cheap, and so find many buyers, and to sell dear to such as could not buy elsewhere, and so gain a large profit. The progress of society generally enables nations to produce cheaper; the almost ever injudicious protection of government often gives them means of selling dearer.

The low price of workmanship is the first cause of manufacturing profit; but this low price is never a national advantage, except when it is produced by superiority of climate, greater fertility of soil, or abundance of provision. On the contrary, when it arises from the difficulty of communication, which prevents cultivators from reaping all the profit of their wares, it can only be regarded as a private advantage, acquired at the expense of the national advantage. When the low price of workmanship arises from the poverty of day-labourers, forced by competition to content themselves with what is necessary for life; though commerce may profit by the circumstance, it is nothing better than a national calamity.

Abundance of capital, and the consequence of this, a low price of interest, likewise doubly contribute to diminish the price of production. With more capital, the manufacturer and merchant transact their purchases and sales at a more favourable moment; they are not pressed by either operation, or compelled to provide for the print by a sacrifice of future advantage. Executing all kinds of labour more on the great scale, they save time, and all those incidental charges, which are the same for a great and for a small sum. But as to the saving made by the merchant on the interest of money, it is made at the expense of a particular class, deriving their revenue from trade; it does not enrich the nation any more than the diminution of wages enriched it; it only gives to one what it takes from another.

The increasing division of labour forms, as we have seen, the chief cause of increase in its productive powers; each makes better what he is constantly engaged in making, and when, at length, his whole labour is reduced to the simplest operation, he comes to perform it with such ease and rapidity, that the eye cannot make us comprehend how the address of man should arrive at such precision and promptitude. Often also this division leads to the discovery, that as the workman is now worth nothing more than a machine, a machine may in fact supply his place. Several important inventions in mechanics applied to the arts, have thus sprung from the division of labour; but, by the influence of this division, man has lost in intelligence all that he has gained in the power of producing

71

wealth.

It is by the variety of its operations that our soul is unfolded; it is to procure citizens that a nation wishes to have men, not to procure machines At for operations a little more complicated than those performed by fire or water. The division of labour has conferred a value on operations so simple, that children, from the tenderest age, are capable of executing them; and children, before having developed any of their faculties, before having experienced any enjoyment of life, are accordingly condemned to put a wheel in motion, to turn a spindle, to empty a bobbin. More lace, more pins, more threads, and cloth of cotton or silk, are the fruit of this great division of labour; but how dearly have we purchased them, if it is by this moral sacrifice of so many millions of human beings!

The employment of machinery in place of men, has contributed generally to lessen the price of production. At the renovation of arts and civilization, there was so much work to be done, and so few hands to do it; oppression had so far reduced the poor class; there remained so much uncultivated land in the country; so many ill-supplied trades in towns; and sovereigns required so many soldiers for war, that it seemed workmanship could never be economized enough, since an artisan, sent away from one trade, would always find ten others ready to receive him. Circumstances are not now the same; our labour is scarcely sufficient for the labourers. We shall endeavour, in another place, to explain the cause of this fact; in the mean time, surely none will maintain that it can be advantageous to substitute a machine for a man, if this man cannot find work elsewhere; or that it is not better to have the population composed of citizens than of steam-engines, even though the cotton cloth of the first should be a little dearer than that of the second.

The application of science to art is not limited to the invention of machinery; its result is the discovery of raw materials, dyeing ingredients, preservative methods more sure and economical. It has produced better work at a cheaper rate; it has protected the health of labourers, as well as their produce; and its effect in augmenting wealth has almost always been beneficial to humanity.

Finally, the different quarters of the globe possess advantages of climate, soil, exposure, which not only render the subsistence of man more easy or cheaper, but also place within his reach certain raw materials, which other nations cannot procure at the same price. Hence results in their favour a kind of monopoly, which they exercise over others, and of which it is rare that they do not take advantage. There is also, in some degree, a natural advantage in the superiority of the people itself, in certain climates; the bounty of nature seems to have reserved for those who inhabit them a superiority of industry, intelligence, strength of body, or constancy in labour, which do not even require to be developed by education.

But other qualities, other virtues, which appear to contribute more effectually still to the increase of riches, as well as to the happiness of society - the love of order, economy, sobriety, justice - are almost always the work of public institutions. Religion, education, government, and principles of honour, change the nature of men; and as they make good or bad citizens of them, they advance or retard their approach to the object proposed by political economy.

But governments have rarely been satisfied with such advantages as the trade of their states might owe to nature, or to the progress of society. They have attempted to favour the increase of commercial wealth; and their different expedients have most frequently tended to assist the merchant in selling dear, rather than producing cheap. With the latter object, however, we have seen the exportation of raw materials prohibited, the rate of interest fixed, and laws enacted to lower the wages of labour.

These three expedients had a common fault, that of sacrificing one class to another, and founding the profit of trade, not on the advantage of consumers, but on the loss of cultivators, capitalists, or workmen; so that its profits, far from being an increase of the national wealth, were a displacement of it. The raw materials on which the arts operate, are all, or nearly all, produced by agriculture or at least drawn from the ground; hence they form part of the proprietor's or the cultivator's wealth. If some advantage did not arise from exporting them, nobody would think of forbidding them to be exported. This prohibition indicates sufficiently, that the persons who produced them were better paid, or gained more by selling them to strangers; and the law restricts their market, in opposition to the principle which we have pointed out above, as the foundation of commercial interest; the principle of obtaining for each article of produce the highest possible price. From such prohibitions to export, there must result, first, a diminution in the price of the raw material, for its price is no longer kept up by free trade; secondly, a diminution in the quantity produced, because it is regulated by the interior demand; and lastly, a deterioration of its quality, for a calling which is ill rewarded, is likewise ill attended to. This, therefore, is one of the most injudicious means of favouring trade; and at the same time, it sacrifices the income of all those who contribute to produce the raw material. Whatever trade gains from them, cannot be considered as adding aught to the national revenue.

To fix the interest of money, or to suppress it altogether, as some legislators have attempted, has, generally been the consequence of religious prejudices, and of mad attempts to adapt the Jewish legislation to modern Europe. The effect of these laws, so opposite to the general interest, has always been either to force contractors to envelop themselves in a secrecy which they must require payment for, and may use as a snare for the unsuspiciousness of others; or else to force capitalists to employ, in other counties, that capital which they could not lend in their own neighborhood, with the same safety and advantage. But the very end which legislators proposed was bad; a diminution in the rent of the national capital, is a national evil; it is a loss of part of the revenue. Most frequently, indeed, this evil is the sign of an advantage greatly superior to it, namely, the increase of capitals themselves; but, in forcibly producing the sign, we cannot at all forcibly produce the thing, any more than by turning round the pointers of a watch we can alter the flight of time.

Attempts on the part of government to fix the rate of wages, to make workmen labour at a lower price, are ever the most impolitic and the most unjust of these partial laws. If government should propose, as an object, the advantage of any one class in the nation at the expense of the rest, this class ought to be precisely the class of day-labourers. They are more numerous than any other; and to secure their happiness is to make the greatest portion of the nation happy. They have fewer enjoyments than any other; they obtain less advantage than any other from the constitution of society; they produce wealth, and themselves obtain scarcely any share of it. Obliged to struggle for subsistence with their employers, they are not a match for them in strength. Masters and workmen are indeed mutually necessary to each other; but the necessity weighs daily on the workman; it allows respite to his master. The first must work that he may live, the second may wait and live for a time without employing workmen. Hence in the riots and combinations of workmen for obtaining an increase of wages, their conduct is often violent and tumultuous, and often merits the chastisement which it never fails to receive; but scarcely an instance exists, where justice has not been upon their side.

The expedients invented by governments to assist their merchants in selling dear, are numerous. Some tend to diminish the number of producers in a market of given extent, and therefore to force buyers to raise their price; such are apprenticeships, corporations, monopolies granted to companies, prohibitions to import, exclusive governments of colonies, and favours obtained by treaties of commerce; others, such as bounties and drawbacks, are destined really to extend the market; though, by securing to the manufacturer a profit at the government's expense, not the consumer's.

The regulations of apprenticeships and the statutes of corporations, were destined, it is said, to hinder ignorant workmen from following any trade which they did not yet understand; they were forced to devote a determinate number of years to learn it, and afterwards to gain admission into a body which always made obstacles to the entrance of new comers, and limited their number. The pretence of thus watching over the training of artisans cannot be made good. It has often been proved, that rivalship alone gives that training, whilst a long apprenticeship blunts the mind and discourages industry; but the true, though secret object, to diminish the number of those exercising a trade, was attained. The corporate body exercised a kind of monopoly against the consumer; it took care at all times to keep the supply below the demand. The merchant doubtless gained more; but he gained on a smaller production. There was less work done, less increase of capital, less population supported; and as to the merchant's extraordinary profit, it was compensated by an equal loss to the consumer, who was obliged to pay, not according to his own advantage or convenience, but according to the arbitrary caprice of a corporation which gave laws to him.

In all trading counties, a more or less exclusive monopoly has been granted, on certain occasions, to some associations of merchants, under the name of Trading Companies. The avowed motive for sacrificing the whole class to this privileged number was the particular nature of the trade thus subjected to a monopoly, which trade it was said could not be supported except by very extensive funds; but governments had often a secret motive besides; and this was, the sum of money for which the merchants bought their privilege. A company's monopoly has never failed to heighten the price for the consumer, to diminish production and consumption, to give the national capital a false direction; sometimes by attracting it prematurely to a branch of trade which was not yet suitable, sometimes by repelling it when fruitlessly seeking an employment. But although companies obtained the desired privilege of buying cheap and selling dear, by nature they are so ill suited for economy and trading speculations, that although amazingly rich, and sometimes sovereigns of counties, these companies, their administrators having no immediate interest in the prosperity of their trust, have almost all been robbed, and very few of them have not ended in bankruptcy.

These different expedients for the protection of commerce, are now generally decried, though almost all governments yet agree in repelling from their states the produce of foreign manufactories, or at least in loading it with heavy duties, to give the national produce an advantage. The prohibitive system of custom-house duties plainly gives to a growing manufactory an advantage equivalent to the largest bounty. Perhaps this manufactory scarcely produces the hundredth part of what the nation consumes of such commodities; but the hundred purchasers must compete with each other to obtain the one seller's preference, and the ninety-nine rejected by him will be compelled to obtain goods by smuggling. In this case, the nation's loss will be as a hundred; its gain as one. Whatever advantage may arise from giving a new manufacture to a nation, certainly there are few which deserve such a sacrifice and even these might always be set a-going by less expensive means. Besides, we must also take into account the weighty inconveniences of establishing the vexatious system of duties, of covering the frontiers with an army of customhouse officers, and with another not less dangerous army of smugglers, and thus of training the subjects to disobedience. We must remember, above all, that it is not the interest of a nation to produce every thing indifferently; that it ought to confine its efforts to such goods or commodities as it can manufacture at the cheapest rate; or to such as, whatever price they cost, are essential to its safety. It ought to be recollected that each merchant knows his own business better than government can do; that the whole nation's productive power is limited; that in a given time, it has but a given number of hands, and a given quantity of capital; that by forcing it to enter upon a kind of work which it did not previously execute, we almost always at the same time force it to abandon a kind of work which it did execute: whilst the most probable result of such a change is the abandonment of a more lucrative manufacture for another which is less so, and which personal interest had designedly overlooked.

If the prohibitive system gives a very powerful, though very expensive encouragement to rising manufactures, it can offer, in regard to such, no advantage to those which are already prosperous; the sacrifice at least which it imposes on consumers, is entirely useless. If the manufacture was destined for exportation, government, by granting a monopoly of the interior market, causes it to abandon its ancient habits to assume others which probably are less advantageous. Every manufacture destined for exportation gives proof of not fearing the competition of foreigners. From the moment that it can support competition abroad, notwithstanding the expense of transport, it has still less reason to dread this competition in the very place of production. Thus nothing is more common than to see goods prohibited which never could have been imported with advantage, and which gained credit solely by being so prohibited.

By the prohibitive system, governments had proposed to increase the number and productive powers of their manufactures. It is doubtful if they rightly knew the price they paid for this advantage, and the prodigious sacrifices they imposed on consumers, their subjects, to bring into existence an unborn class of producers; but they succeeded much more rapidly even than speculators on political economy expected. For a time they excited the bitterest complaints on the part of consumers; but even these complaints ceased afterwards, because sacrifices in fact had also ceased, and manufactures so powerfully encouraged, had soon provided with profusion for the national wants. But this emulation of all governments to establish manufactures every where, has produced two strange and unexpected effects on the commercial system of Europe; one is the disproportionate increase of production without any relation to consumption; the other is the effort of each nation to live isolated, to suffice for itself, and refuse every kind of foreign trade.

Before governments had been seized with this manufacturing ardour, the establishment of a new manufacture had always to struggle with a crowd of national habits and prejudices, which form as it were the vis inertiae of the human mind. To overcome this force, it was necessary to offer speculators a very manifest advantage; hence a new species of industry could scarcely arise without a distinct previous demand, and the market was always found before the manufacture destined to occupy it. Governments, in their zeal, have not proceeded upon this principle; they have ordered stockings and hats beforehand, reckoning that legs and heads would be found afterwards. They have seen their people well and economically clothed by strangers, and yet have caused them to produce clothes in the country itself. During war, this new production was not capable of being too exactly appreciated; but when peace came, it was found that all things had been made in double quantity; and the readier the mutual communication of states had become, the more embarrassed were they to dispose of all their works executed without orders.

Consumers who at the beginning had been satisfied, afterwards found themselves called to unexpected gains, because merchants, eager to recover their funds, were forced to sell a very great quantity of goods with loss. Manufacturers gave the signal for these sacrifices; resigning themselves to a cruel loss of their capital, they induced extensive merchants to furnish themselves with goods beyond their custom or ability, in order to profit by what appeared a good opportunity. Several of the latter have been forced to experience a similar loss, before their excessive supply could be introduced to the shops of retail dealers; and these again before they could make them be accepted by consumers. A universal embarrassment was felt by manufacturers, merchants, and retailers, and this was followed by the annihilation of the capital destined to support industry. The fruit of long saving and long labour was lost in a year. Consumers have gained certainly, but their gain is scarcely perceptible even to themselves. By laying up a stock of goods for several years to profit by their cheapness, they have also included themselves in the general embarrassment, and still farther retarded the period when the balance can be re-established between consumption and production.

According to the former organization of Europe, all states did not make pretences to all kinds of industry. Some had attached themselves to agriculture, others to navigation, others to manufactures; and the condition of these latter, even in prosperous times, could not have appeared so worthy of envy as to demand prodigious efforts to attain it. A miserable and degraded population almost always produced these rich stuffs; these elegant ornaments, this furniture which it was never destined to enjoy and if the men who directed these unhappy workmen sometimes raised immense fortunes, those fortunes were as frequently destroyed. The development of nations proceeds naturally in all directions; it is scarcely ever prudent to obstruct it, but it is no less dangerous to hasten it; and the governments of Europe, by having of all hands attempted to force nations, are at the present day loaded with a population, which they have created by requiring superfluous labour, and which they know not how to save from the horrors of famine.

The existence of this manufacturing population, and the duty of providing for its wants, have constrained governments to alter the aim of their legislation. Formerly, in the real spirit of the mercantile system, they encouraged manufactures, in order to sell much to foreigners, and grow rich at their expense; now, perceiving that a prohibitive system is every where adopted, or like to be adopted, they cannot any longer count on the custom of strangers, and therefore study to find, in their own kingdom, consumers for their own workmen; in other words, to become isolated and sufficient for themselves. The system of policy at present, more or less strictly followed by all the nations of Europe, destroys all the advantages of commerce; it hinders each nation from profiting by the superiorities due to its climate, to its soil, to its situation, to the peculiar character of its people; it arms man against man, and breaks the tie which was destined to sooth national prejudices, and accelerate the civilization of the world.

According to the natural progress of increasing wealth, when capitals are yet inconsiderable, it is certainly desirable to direct them rather to some neighbouring branch of trade, than to one which is very remote; and as the trade of exportation and importation gives foreigners one half of its profit, and the natives another, a country which has little capital may desire to employ it entirely in the trade of its interior, or for its own use; and the more so, because if the market is near the producer, the same capital will be several times renewed in a given period, whilst another capital, destined for a foreign market, will scarcely accomplish a single renewal. But the capitalist's interest will always direct him with certainty, in such cases to do what suits the country best; because his profit is proportioned to the need there is of it, and consequently to the direction in which the public demand carries him.

Besides, nations, on reckoning up their produce and their wants, almost constantly forget that neighboring foreigners are much more convenient and more advantageous producers and consumers than distant countrymen. The relation of markets on the two banks of the Rhine is much more important, both for the German and the French merchant, than the relation of markets between the Palatinate and Brandenburgh is for the former, or between Alsace and Provence for the latter.

The ardour, with which all governments have excited every species of production, by means of their restrictive system, has brought about such a disproportion between labour and demand, that perhaps it has become necessary for every state to think first, not of the comfort, but of the existence of its subjects, and to maintain those barriers which have been so imprudently erected. An important part of the population might, perhaps, be cut off by penury, in the course of a few years; and it is reasonable that each state should seek to preserve itself and those depending on it from such a calamity. Yet, we cannot without pain, behold the rivetting of this anti-social system, and the abandonment of that ancient spirit of commerce, which triumphed over barbarism, and taught hostile hordes to know and esteem each other.

Governments, after having attempted to give the national producers a monopoly in their own country, have sometimes endeavoured to procure them a similar advantage in foreign countries, by treaties of commerce. Such actions, always subordinate to policy, granted to a favoured nation an exemption from some part of the duties required from others, on consideration of some reciprocal advantage. It cannot be doubted that such an exemption was advantageous to the nation in whose favour it was granted; but, on the other hand, it was just as disadvantageous to the nation granting it; and when a treaty of commerce bore a concession of mutual exemption, each state should have discovered, that a monopoly granted to its producers was too dearly purchased by a monopoly granted to foreigners, against its consumers: and the more so, as there existed no kind of relation between the two favoured branches of trade. Some show of reason may be discovered, why the consumers of cloth should be taxed for the advantage of cloth manufacturers; but there is no shallow of reason why the consumers of wine in England should experience a loss, in compensation for an advantage to the sellers of goods in Portugal.

No treaty of commerce can fully satisfy the greediness of merchants desiring a monopoly; and therefore governments invented the fanatic expedient of creating in a colony a nation expressly to be purchasers from their merchants. The colonists were prohibited from establishing any manufacture at home, that so they might be more dependent on the mother country.

They were carefully prevented from following any species of foreign trade; they were subjected to regulations the most vexatious, and contrary to their own interests; not for the mother country's good, but for the good of a small number of merchants. The infinite advantages attached to a new country, where every kind of labour is profitable, because every thing is yet to do, enabled colonies to prosper, although they were continually sacrificed. As their raw produce was fit for a distant trade, they had it in their power to support a most unequal exchange, in which nothing was taken from them that the buyer could procure at home; but their rapid increase itself bears witness against the system which has founded them; they have prospered by a system diametrically opposite to that followed by the mother country. The exportation of all raw produce, the importation of all wrought produce, has been encouraged in colonies, and have presented to such as believe in the existence, and calculate the state, of a commercial balance, a result as disadvantageous for themselves, as it was advantageous for the mother country. Doubtless, their oppression gave the latter all the profits of a monopoly; yet, in a very circumscribed market; whilst the free trade of all Europe, with all its colonies, would have been more advantageous for both, by infinitely extending the market of the one, and accelerating the progress of the other. What justice and policy should have taught, force will obtain, and the colonial system cannot long continue.

Governments, in the last place, to favour commerce, have granted it bounties and drawbacks. A bounty is a reward which the state decrees to the manufacturer, on account of his goods, which comes to him in the shape of profit. A drawback is a restitution of all the taxes, which a piece of goods had paid, granted to it at the moment of its exportation. A drawback is perfectly just and reasonable. It leaves the national producer, in the foreign market, on a footing of equality with all his rivals, whilst, if beforehand be had paid a tax in his own country, he could not have sustained the competition. Bounties are the strangest encouragements which a government can give. They may be justified when granted for the fabrication of an article, the production of which it is necessary to procure at any price: but when granted on exported goods, as often happens, government pays merchants, at the expense of its own subjects, that foreigners may buy cheaper than them.

Thus, nearly all the favours which governments confer on trade and manufactures, are contrary even to sound policy or justice; and, judging of them by the law of profit and loss, we should infer, that all this attention, bestowed by government on trade, had done more ill than good. But political economy is, in great part, a moral science. After having calculated the interests of men, it ought also to foresee what will act upon their passions. Ruled, as they are, by self-interest, pointing out their advantage will not be sufficient to determine their pursuit of it. Nations have sometimes need of being shaken, as it were, to be roused from their torpor. The small weight which would suffice to incline the balance, with a calculating people, is not sufficient when that balance is rusted by prejudice and long continued habits. In such a case, a skilful administration must occasionally submit to allow a real and calculable loss, in order to destroy an old custom, or change a destructive prepossession. When rooted prejudices have abandoned to disrespect every useful and industrious profession, when a nation thinks there can be no dignity except in noble indolence; when even men of science themselves, carried away by public opinion, blush at the useful applications made of their discoveries, and in such applications see nothing but what they call the cookery of their sciences; it perhaps becomes necessary to grant favours, altogether extraordinary, to the industry which it is necessary to create, to fix incessantly the thoughts of a too lively people on the career of fortune which lies before them, intimately to connect the discoveries of science with those of art, and to excite the ambition of those who have always lived in idleness, by fortunes so brilliant as, at length, to make them think of what may be accomplished by their wealth and their activity.

It is true, the mercantile capital of a nation is limited in a given time, and those who dispose of it, always desiring to put it out to the greatest advantage, have no need of any new stimulant to augment it, or turn it into the channels where it best produces profit. But all the capital of a nation is not mercantile. Inclination to idleness, which public institutions have fostered among certain nations, not only binds men, but also fetters fortunes. The same indolence, which makes those people lose their time, makes them also lose their money. The annual revenue of territorial fortunes forms of itself an immense capital, which may be added to or deducted from the sum devoted to support industry. In southern counties, the whole revenue of the nobility was annually dissipated in useless pomp; but to recall the heads of noble families into activity has likewise been found sufficient to give them habits of economy. The great French or Italian proprietor, becoming manufacturer has, at once, given a useful direction to the revenue of his land, by adding his own activity to that of a nation becoming more industrious, and added likewise all the power of his wealth, which formerly lay unemployed.

The torpor of a nation may sometimes be so great, that the clearest demonstration of advantages, which it might derive from a new species of industry, shall never induce it to make the attempt. Example, alone, can then awake self-interest. French industry has found, in the single little state of Lucca, more than ten new branches, to employ itself upon, with great advantage both for the country and those who engaged in them. The most absolute liberty was not sufficient to direct attention to these objects. The zeal and activity of the princess Eliza, who called into her little sovereignty several head-manufacturers, who furnished them with money and houses, who brought the produce of their shops into fashion, has founded a more durable prosperity in a decaying city, and restored to a beneficent activity much capital and intellect, which, but for her, would forever have remained unemployed.

When government means to protect commerce, it often acts with precipitation, in complete ignorance of its true interests; almost always with despotic violence, which tramples under foot the greater part of private arrangements; and almost always with an absolute forgetfulness of the advantage of consumers, who, as they form by far the most numerous class, have more right than any other to confound their well-being with that of the nation. Yet it must not be inferred, that government never does good to trade. It is government which can give habits of dissipation or economy; which can attach honour or discredit to industry and activity; which can turn the attention of scientific men to apply their discoveries to the arts: government is the richest of all consumers; it encourages manufactures by the mere circumstance of giving them its custom. If to this indirect influence it join the care of rendering all communications easy; of preparing roads, canals, bridges; of protecting property, of securing a fair administration of justice; if it do not overload its subjects with taxation in levying the taxes, it adopt no disastrous system, - it will effectually have served commerce, and its beneficial influence will counterbalance many false measures, many prohibitory laws, in spite of which, and not by reason of which, commerce will continue to increase under it.

Chapter 5: Of Money

Wealth incessantly circulates from producers to consumers, by means of money. All kinds of exchange are accomplished under this form, whether the means of producing wealth are transmitted from one proprietor to another, or when land or movable capital changes its owner, or when labour is sold, or when the object destined to be consumed reaches the hands that are to use it. Money facilitates all these exchanges; it occurs among the different contractors as a thing which all desire, and by means of which every one may find what he immediately requires; as a thing, moreover, submitted to invariable calculation, and by means of which all other values may be appreciated, this alone being their scale.

Money performs several functions at once: it is the sign of all other values; it is their pledge and also their measure. As a sign, money represents every other kind of wealth; by transmitting it from hand to hand we transmit a right to all other values. It is not money itself which the day-labourer requires; but food, clothing, lodging, of which it is the sign. It is not for money that the manufacturer wishes to exchange his produce, but for raw materials, that he may again begin to work; and for objects of consumption, that he may begin to enjoy. It is not money which the capitalist lends the merchant to profit by; it is all that the merchant will purchase with this money immediately afterwards; for so long as the merchant keeps it in the original shape, he can draw no advantage from it, and his capital will not begin its course of production till the money is out of his hands. By an abuse of language, which has caused much error and confusion, the words money and capital have become almost synonymous: money indeed represents all other capital, but it is itself the capital of no man; it is always barren by nature, and wealth does not begin to increase, till after money has left the hands of its possessor.

Money is not only the sign of wealth, it is also the

pledge of it. It not only represents wealth, it contains the worth of it. Like wealth, it has been produced by a labour which it wholly compensates. In work and advances of all sorts employed in extracting it from the mine, it has cost a value equal to what it passes for in the world. It furnishes to trade a commodity which is expensive; because purchased like every other, it is the sole kind of wealth which is not increased by circulation, or dissipated by enjoyment. It issues, still without alteration from the hands of him who employs it usefully, and of him who squanders it upon his pleasures. But the high price at which society acquires money, though at first view it appears an inconvenience, is precisely what gives it the merit of being an imperishable pledge for its possessors. As its value was not given by arbitrary convention, arbitrary convention cannot take its value away. It may be more or less sought after according as it occurs more or less abundantly in the market; but its price can never deviate very far from what would be required to extract an equal quantity from the mine.

Money, in the last place, is a common measure of values. Before the invention of money, it must have been very difficult to compare the value of a bag of corn with that of a yard of cloth. Dress was equally necessary with food; but the processes by which men procured them, seemed scarcely susceptible of being compared. Money has furnished a common and invariable unity to which every thing can be referred. Nations, who are not acquainted with the use of metals, have, nevertheless, so felt the advantages of this common measure that they have formed an ideal unity, to which they refer every kind of value.

The important part which money performs in political economy, and the various properties by which it animates exchanges, and protects and serves to measure them, explain the illusion which has misled, not only the vulgar, but even the greater part of statesmen, and exhibited this commodity in their eyes as the efficient cause of labour, and the creator of all wealth. It is essential for us, however, to pause here, that we

88

may both display those errors in a clear point of view, and firmly demonstrate the principles which follow. In the epoch of civilization, at which we are arrived, no labour can be accomplished without a capital to set it in motion; but this capital, though almost constantly represented by money, is yet quite a different thing. An increase of the national capital is the most powerful encouragement to labour; but an increase in the circulating medium has not of necessity the same effect. Capitals co-operate powerfully in the annual reproduction of wealth, giving rise to an annual revenue; but money continues barren, and gives rise to no revenue. Indeed, the competition between those capitals, which are offered to accomplish the annual labour of the nation, forms the basis for the interest of money; but the greater or less abundance of the circulating medium, has no influence in the fixing of this interest.

Painful experience has shown all the inhabitants of Europe what a dearth was, and a period of general penury among a civilized people. At these mournful epochs, every one has heard it a hundred times observed, that it was not corn or food which was wanting, but money. Indeed, vast magazines of corn have often remained full till the next harvest; those provisions, if proportionably shared among the people, would have almost always been sufficient for their support; but the poor, having no money to offer, were not able to buy them; they could not, in exchange for their labour, obtain money, or at least enough of it, to subsist. Money was wanting, natural wealth superabundant. What phenomenon could appear more proper to confirm the universal prejudice which looks for wealth in money, not in consumable capital?

But the money, which is wanting in a time of scarcity, is the wage offered to the workman to make him labour. the wage, by means of which, he would have purchased a subsistence. The workmen never labour, except when some of those who have accumulated capitals, or in other words, the fruit of preceding labours, can profit from those capitals, by furnishing, on one hand, the raw material, on the other, a subsistence for the artisan. Labour cannot be carried on so as to produce any material fruit, any fruit capable of becoming wealth, without raw materials on which to operate; the workman cannot labour without food to support him; and, therefore, every kind of labour is impossible without a capital previously existing in objects of consumption, to furnish his materials and his wages; and, if the workman himself lay out these advances, it is because he combines for this little object, the two characters of capitalist and artisan.

As the workman requires a capitalist, so the capitalist requires workmen; because his capital will be unproductive if it continue idle; and the revenue which he expects and has to live upon springs from the labour which he causes to be executed. Hence, whenever he is occupied in a productive enterprise, he employs all his capital in causing labour, and leaves no part of it in idleness. If he is a cloth-maker, and has devoted ten thousand pounds to his manufacture, he does not stop till his ten thousand pounds are done, and he no longer has new sums to employ in the operation. If it be then asked why he stops, he will answer, like the workman, that money is wanting, that money does not circulate.

It is not, however, money which is then wanting any more than in the former case; it is consumption, or the consumer's revenue. On commencing his manufacture, the capitalist studied to adjust it to the demand; and he reckoned that as soon as his cloths should be ready, they would be purchased by consumers, whose money, the sign of their revenue, would replace his capital, and become the sign of subsistence to new workmen, to whom he would pay new wages. It is not money which the consumer is in want of, but revenue. Some have had inferior harvests this year; some have gained a smaller interest on their capitals, a smaller share on the annual re-production of the fruits of industry; others, who have no income but what arises from their labour, have not found employment; or else the whole three classes are not poorer than they were, but the manufacturer had imagined them to be richer, and regulated his production according to an income which does not exist.

Income, of which we have seen all the different sources in the second chapter, is a material and consumable thing; it springs from labour; it is destined for enjoyment; it is exactly of the same nature with the advances in wages and raw material laid out by the manufacturer; and money is but the sign and the measure of it. The capital it should replace is also composed of material objects, destined for consumption, and incessantly renewed. Money serves but to represent it, and always forms the smallest part of each merchant's funds. We have supposed the cloth-maker to possess 100,000 l.; but, it half this sum is employed in fixed capitals, it will be sufficient, if his sale amount weekly to 1200 l. to give him, in the shape of interest and profit, 20 per cent. on his circulating capital, and to allow 1000 l weekly, in money, to maintain an annual production of 60,000 l.; so that he never possesses in cash more than the fiftieth part of his circulating capital.

An increase of the national capitals is the most powerful encouragement of labour; either because this augmentation presupposes an augmentation of income, and, consequently, of means of consumption; or because these capitals, not being profitable to their proprietor, except as they are employed, each capitalist incessantly endeavours to create new production by their means. In distributing them to his workmen, he gives to those workmen revenue which enables them to purchase and consume the preceding year's production; and he sees those capitals return increased by the revenue, which he is to expect from them in the following year's production. But though he distributes and afterwards recovers them, by means of the circulating medium, which serves for all exchanges, it is not the circulating medium which forms the essential requisite in his operation. The same cloth-maker, labouring each year on an equal quantity, sends 2400 pieces of cloth to the market, which have been valued at 60,000 l. or 25 l. a piece. He exchanges 400 pieces for such objects of consumption as are needed to supply the wants, the enjoyments, the luxuries of himself and family. He exchanges 2000 pieces for the raw materials, and the labour which, within the year, are to re-produce an equal quantity; and thus next year, and every following year, he will have, as before, 2400 pieces to exchange on the same conditions. His capital, equally with his revenue, is actually in cloths, not in money; and the perpetual result of his commerce is to exchange cloth against cloth.

If the consumption of cloth is increased, if by this means his trade, in place of comprehending 2400 pieces annually, comprehends 3000, more labour will, no doubt, be ordered by him, and executed by his workmen; but if the money alone is increased, and not the consumption or the income which determines it, labour and production cannot increase. Let us take separately each one of his customers, as he calls them. There is not one of them who does nor levy a greater or a smaller portion of his income in kind, but all may arrange matters so as to receive the whole of it in money. They are not, however, more rich on this account; they will not be at more expense; they will not buy more cloth from him, and this trade will experience no kind of augmentation. What happens to individuals may equally happen to nations. The revenue of a country or the sum total of profits arising from the different kinds of labour, amounted, we shall say, last year, and this year, to fifty millions; but last year the country levied all its profit in goods, in merchandise destined for its consumption; this year, from some mercantile circumstance, some arrangement of exchanges, it has levied the fourth, the third part, in money imported through the frontiers. It is neither richer nor poorer, for this alteration; its consumption will, as formerly, be fifty millions; and with regard to the money imported, apparently its industry required this money, otherwise it will be again exported. To increase the circulating medium of a country, without increasing its capital, without increasing its revenue, without increasing its consumption is to do nothing for its prosperity, nothing for the encouragement of labour.

Since no labour can be accomplished without a capital to set it in motion; since no re-production of wealth can take place without raw materials for the work, and subsistence for the workmen, it follows that the furnisher of those wages and materials has taken the most intimate share in the re-production; he is, in a great degree, the author of its profits, and has the most evident right to participate in them. But he who lends a capital lends nothing else but those wages and raw materials represented by money. He lends a thing eminently productive, or rather the only one which is productive; for since all wealth proceeds from labour, and all labour is put in motion by its wage, he lends labour itself, or the first cause of production in all kinds of wealth. Hence, whenever an odious sense has been attached to the word usury, meaning by it any kind of interest paid for the use of a sum of money, under pretext that as money produced no fruit, there could be no lawful share of profit where there was no profit; in this case, an absurd distinction has been formed. There was just as much reason to prohibit the renting of land, or the wages of labour, because without a capital to put land and labour in exercise, both would remain unfruitful.

Theologians, however, were right in saying that gold and silver were barren by nature: they are barren so long as kept in their own shape; they cease to be barren, the instant they become the sign of another kind of wealth, which is emphatically productive. Theologians, if they determined to abide by the single principle on which their prohibition was founded, should have been contented with declaring usury criminal, every time the lender obliged the borrower to keep the deposit in its primary form, locked up in a strong box, from the moment of borrowing to that of payment. For it is quite certain that money, whilst locked up, produces no fruit; and neither borrower, nor lender can get good of it except by parting with it.

But, if money is of itself barren; it produces no fruit but in so far as it is the sign of other values, then it is evident that no good can be done by multiplying the sign and not the thing. It is true, if you multiply the sign in a single country, you give this

93

country the means of commanding the thing, provided that thing be found in any, country. but when you multiply the sign in all countries at once, you do nothing for any. At present, there exists such a proportion between the sign and the thing, that a pound sterling is worth a bag of corn; but if, by the stroke of a magic rod, you should instantly double all the money in the world, since every thing to be obtained in exchange would continue the same, two pounds in place of one would be required to represent a bag of corn. The quantity of corn consumed by a workman, in food, would not be altered, consequently his wage must be doubled. With twice as many guineas, exactly the same work would be done, and nothing would be changed but names and numbers.

Capitalists require their capital to be employed, that it may gain a revenue; and hence they offer it for a certain price, to such as wish to cause labour; workmen, on the other hand, and those who employ workmen, have need of capital for their labour; and, after reckoning up the profit expected from it, they offer a certain share of their advantage to capitalists. The necessities of money-lenders and of money-borrowers, come thus to a state of equilibrium in all markets; those classes of men agree upon a medium rate. The regulator of their bargain is always the quantity of labour required by consumers, compared with the quantity of capital, representing raw materials and wages, to be disposed of in executing this labour. If the want is great, and the means of labour small, the interest of money will be considerable; if, on the contrary, there is much capital in circulation, and little employment for it, interest will be very low. It must always be regulated by what is called the quantity of money offered in the market, because money is the sign of capital, though not capital itself. Far from being augmented by the magical increase of money above alluded to, capital would not even be increased by the arrival of money, in great abundance, at a particular place of trade, without losing any thing of its value in comparison with the things it purchases; and no change in the rate of interest would result from this circumstance.

Nearly all the circulating capital of each manufacturer and trader is successively presented to him under the shape of money, in its return from the buyer to the seller; but the part of his funds, which a merchant actually has in money, forms, in ordinary cases, but a small portion of the capital employed in his commerce; an infinitely greater portion being kept in its original state in his own warehouses, or in those of his debtors. On the other hand, it is almost always in the power of each merchant instantaneously to augment the quantity of money at his disposal, by selling his goods at a less profit, or by discounting the debts which are owed him. In this way, he has money when he pleases, without being richer; the money, far from adding to his capital, is purchased with it. If such operations are performed at one time by several merchants in the same town, that town purchases money from its neighbours; if by a great number of French, English, or German merchants, we say that France, England, or Germany purchases money. There will, in reality, be found much more in the markets to make payments with; guineas will be much more abundant; but there will be neither more nor fewer deposits offered to lend, and the rate of interest will not be any way affected by the change. Such as are acquainted with the movements of trading places, know well that guineas may abound in them while capitals are scarce, or guineas be scarce while capitals abound.

It is a gross error, then, to believe, that, in all cases, a considerable importation of the circulating medium will make the rate of interest fall, or an exportation make it rise. Money is a kind of wealth; and like any other kind of wealth, it forms part of the circulating capital. If the money imported is a gift, or a tribute; if it costs nothing to the nation, it will certainly augment its circulating capital, and must certainly contribute to lower the rate of interest on the spot; but the same sums paid to the nation in goods would equally contribute to that end. If, on the other hand, this money has been purchased with any other portion of the capital, in that case the sum total of the latter will remain the same, and the rate of interest will not be affected.

Upon these principles, it is easy to see how mines of silver and gold do not enrich a nation more than any other kind of industry. The precious metals drawn from the mine are goods purchased, like all other goods, at the price of labour and capital. The opening of the mine, the construction of its galleries, the establishment of refining furnaces, require large advances, independently of the labour by which the ore is drawn from the bowels of the earth. This labour, and its fruits, may be exactly paid by the metal produced, and the state will gain by the operation, as by any other manufacture. But, in general, the profits of mines are irregular. As the head prize in a lottery seduces gamesters, an unlooked for advantage encourages miners to continue their exertions, although the usual returns be inferior to those obtained by any other kind of industry; and nearly all of them are ruined, just like gamesters, because they were at first successful.

From these principles, we may also conclude, that the blame so frequently imputed to Frederic II and the Canton of Berne for having hoarded up and withdrawn from the country a large portion of the natural circulating medium, is without foundation. By saving a part of their expenses, they, of course, in some degree, diminished consumption and re-production; by preserving some millions in their coffers, they in some degree diminished the circulating capital: but the money locked up by them was soon replaced by other moneys which the country purchased; and, besides, the whole circulating medium of a nation is so small, compared with its whole circulating capital, that such a void can never be considered as a national misfortune, or counterbalance the immense advantage of possessing a fund ready, without new sacrifices, at the moment of want.

From confounding money with capital, has arisen the general mistake of attempting to increase the national capital by a fictitious capital, which, not having been created by an expensive labour, is not, like gold or silver, a pledge of the values it represents; and which, after having delighted nations with the illusions of wealth, has so frequently left them in ruin.

It will be more easy to follow the operation, by which so many states in our time have endeavoured to replace their money by paper, if we previously direct our attention to the manner in which one of the most ancient trading cities of France made a few crowns perform the functions of a considerable circulating medium. At Lyons, it was agreed upon in trade, that all payments should take place only at four fixed periods, quarterly. During the three days which the payments took up, all the accounts of the city were settled at once. Each, at the same period, had much to receive and much to pay. But, on the days immediately preceding the payments, all the merchants used to meet on the exchange, to make what they called viremens; in other words, to assign, one to another, such sums as would settle their accounts. A owed B, who owed C, who owed D, who owed E, himself indebted to A; and the five accounts were settled without any payment. If E was not indebted to A, it was agreed that A should pay E, and the other four were acquitted by a single payment. Every merchant bought but to sell again; received, therefore, but to pay; and if those assignments were extended to their utmost limits, one single sum of ten thousand pounds would probably settle all the transactions of a city, though these amounted to several millions.

But all mutual debts are not equal, and bankruptcies occasion difficulties, and sometimes errors in the assignments. The invention of banks has supplied this deficiency. The Bank of Amsterdam is a kind of open bar, where assignments may constantly be made. Every trader pays or receives, by a line which is written down in the bank's books, on the debtor or creditor side of his account, without any money being disbursed. Among merchants, who have all an open credit with the bank, the operation of the book-keeper supplies with the utmost ease that of cashier; and no difference of amount, or day of payment, prevents sums from being reciprocally balanced.

A bank like that of Amsterdam, however, is of use only to such as have a current account in it. Many traders may have no account; and few or none who are not traders ever have any, though called, as well as others, to pay and to receive. To extend the advantage of assignments also to the business of such persons, those note-banks were invented which have since become so common in all parts of Europe. Their notes are assignments on the bank, payable to the bearer on demand. Each, by combining several notes, may make his odd payments himself; and hence it is generally most convenient for him to transmit them to others, as he received them, without having drawn any money; and even though each may require payment at his pleasure, no one thinks of it, just because each feeling that he may do it any time, feels always that it will be soon enough afterwards.

Up to that period, banks had done nothing but simplify payments, and save the employment of money, and render circulation easy with a smaller sum than would otherwise have been required. But some one must profit by this saving. In arranging the assignments at Lyons, each profited according to his share in trade; each needed to have money in his coffers only four times yearly, for three days. He, of course, gained interest for the remaining 353 days; and as those assignments simplified all his operations, a smaller sum performed for him the office of a greater. When banks were established, it was they that profited by this saving of money. They received interest, not for the money really given by them, but for the money, which every bearer of notes had it in his power to demand from them, at a moment's notice. This interest of notes, reckoned equal to gold, was a pure advantage for bankers; since the money promised, far from being drawn, had not even remained at the bank, where it would have been barren. Bankers, reckoning on the confidence of the public, had caused it to labour, and recalled it for their payments only as they needed it.

It was by discount on such of the proceeds of trade as were payable at long dates, that banks pushed their notes into circulation. They required an interest for exchanging their paper against that of trade, because theirs was exigible at sight, though it was not really paid before the other. The discount required by the bank served to introduce the interest of money, and to regulate it in the place. Bankers, in virtue of their credit alone, seemed to have capitals of almost immense extent, to offer in the service of merchants. Credit soon appeared to have a creative power, and speculators, persuaded that by emitting a bank one, they added as much to the public wealth as by importing an equal sum of money, delivered their minds to dreams dangerous for themselves, and for the states that gave ear to them. They proposed the establishment of banks to multiply the funds of trade, to provide for the enterprises of agriculture, to set labour every where in motion, to increase the general capital; and redouble the activity of industry.

Governments, on their side, imagined that in banks they had found an open mine, from which they might draw at discretion. At each new season of need, they stuck new bank-notes. But they soon perceived, with astonishment, that notes were no longer received with the same confidence, and were speedily carried back to the bank for payment; and next, as their custom generally is, they substituted their authority for the nature of things. They refused payment on demand, but they ordered each citizen to receive as ready coin, those notes which had thus become paper money; and they authorised every debtor to pay his accounts with it.

The circulation of paper money became, in a short time, nothing less than a general bankruptcy. Notwithstanding all the orders of government, paper fell every day in its proportion to silver or to goods. The bearers of it, feeling that they had no pledge for the values, the sign of which they were always presenting, dreaded lest the paper should undergo a new deterioration in their hands, and made haste to get rid of it. Each lost and caused loss, each having no longer any common measure of value, became unable to distinguish the gain from the loss of his bargain, and always selling with advantage, he ended in ruin. During this time, coin disappeared, goods themselves were exported from the country, without giving any return; and the expedient, which promised to create immense wealth, produced nothing but ruin and confusion.

A fatal error had led to all these misfortunes. It was imagined that credit had the power of creating wealth; whilst, in fact, credit never creates any thing, but merely borrows with one hand to lend with the other, that wealth, which, to be of use, must have previously existed in the state. Paper money can be substituted only for the metallic money already in existence; it is the value of this which it borrows. The banker, who finds credit, acquires the power to dispose of a part of the currency equal to the paper he emits. If he in reality withdraw part of the currency from circulation, his paper will remain there; if he does not withdraw it, others will withdraw it for him, the instant it becomes superfluous. But, if this currency was not in circulation at the moment when his bank-notes were emitted, he could not borrow it. In that case, by giving forced circulation to his paper, he depreciates not only this paper, but all that was already in the hands of the public.

The money of a country has a determinate relation to the wealth of that country, and to the activity with which its wealth circulates. The same guineas serve, in the course of a year, for a great number of different bargains; yet still there is a necessary equation between the mass of values sold, and the sum of guineas which serves to pay them, multiplied by the rapidity of the circulation. If too many guineas exist in the country for the wants of the circulation, this is not a reason why the person holding them in his coffers should keep them longer than he has occasion so to do. All useless stagnation would be so much interest lost for him; and, therefore, he continues still to give them circulation, and some one is always at hand, who, not finding any profitable use to make of them in the country, takes them out of it. If exportation is forbidden, a greater mass of idle guineas will be kept within the country, till the loss of those unable to employ them be great enough to pay the risk of smuggling. If precautions are so well taken that exportation is entirely impossible, the whole money circulated in the country will fall in value till it be reduced to the equation which it cannot pass, that is, to the numerical value of all the sales and payments made within the year, divided by the rapidity of circulation.

In like manner, if the money of a country is not sufficient for its circulation, the country will purchase money in exchange for some one of the values it possesses, just as it would have purchased any other kind of goods. It is not the balance of trade which can make money enter or leave a country. This balance is completely illusory, for it is not true that nations settle their accounts with each other. On the contrary, indeed, it often happens that one is constantly a borrower, the other constantly a lender. And, the credit sales of the most commercial being renewed from year to year - before the first debt is extinguished, a second is already contracted, which is followed by a third; and though each is paid in its turn, the purchaser may nevertheless, perpetually remain debtor to his seller. Thus, sales on credit form a capital which may either increase, or be reimbursed in the inverse sense of other commercial speculations.

Abstracting all that concerns these credits, which modify more than three-fourths of its commercial speculations, the purchases of a nation would be exactly balanced by its sales; because it is as impossible for the one always to purchase, and find the source of a perpetual draining of money, unless it work at mines, as for the other to sell always, and find an employment for a perpetual importation of coined metal. Money is imported, and exported from one nation to another, not because it pays their accounts, but because the one having need of it, sells goods cheaper, till it has acquired enough; and, because the other, having more than enough for its circulation, buys dearer, or, gives a greater quantity of guineas for the same quantity of goods, till the equilibrium is reestablished.

But as the emission of any sum in bank notes, supplies the place of an equal sum of money, the latter is immediately withdrawn from circulation, and sold in foreign countries. So long as there remains any coin to be exported, credit may repeat its operation and create new bank notes; when there is no more coin to export, the paper money, will, of itself, diminishing in value, seek the proper equation; and to whatever nominal sum its fabrication may be carried, it will never sell, in the total amount, for any thing more than the pre-existing total amount of money which it replaces.

Chapter 6: Of Taxation

The primary object of political economy is the development of national wealth; but the object of all governments, since they began to bestow any attention on this subject, has been to participate in this wealth, and to acquire the disposal of a greater share of the nation's annual revenue. The ever increasing necessities of governments, and the excessive expense of wars, have forced princes to load their people with the weightiest possible yoke. Taxation, of itself always an object of repugnance to the subject, has become a nearly intolerable burden; the question is no longer how to make it easy; it is not to do good, but to the least possible evil, that all the efforts of governments in this respect are limited.

Quesnay's sect of economists, who discovered in the net revenue of land the solitary source of wealth, might also believe in the advantage of a solitary species of taxation. They rightly observe, that government, in justice, ought to apply to him who is destined to pay the tax in the long run; because, if this tax is paid by one citizen, reimbursed by a second, who again is reimbursed by a third, not only will there be three persons instead of one incommoded by this payment, but the third will be so much the more incommoded, as it will be necessary for him to indemnify the preceding two for their advances of money. Upon the same principle, the economists called the tax which weighs on the revenue of land a direct tax; to all others they gave the name of indirect, because those taxes arrive indirectly at the person who pays them at last. Their system has fallen, their definitions are no longer admitted, but their denominations have remained in general use.

We have recognised but a single source of wealth, which is labour; yet we have not recognised but a single class of citizens, to whom the revenues produced by labour belong. These are distributed among all the classes of the nation; they assume all manner of forms, and, therefore, it is just that taxation should follow them into all their ramifications. Taxation ought to be considered by the citizens of a state as a recompense for the protection, which government grants to their : persons and properties. It is just that all support this, in proportion to the advantages secured them by society, and to the expenses it incurs for them. The greater part of the charge arising from social establishments, is destined to defend the rich against the poor; because, if left to their respective strength, the former would very speedily be stripped. It is hence just that the rich man contribute not only in proportion to his fortune, but even beyond it, to support a system which is so advantageous to him; in the same way as it is equitable to take from his superfluity rather than from the other's necessaries. Most public labours, most charges for defence and for the administration of justice, have territorial rather than movable property in view; it is hence farther just, that the landed proprietor be taxed in proportion higher than others.

After the sources of income have become various, it cannot be supposed that a single tax will reach them all, unless it assume as a basis this income itself, the valuation of which, in any form, would give room to the most arbitrary and vexatious inquisitions. The tax, though single, would in that case lose all the advantages of simplicity. It was better then, for contributors, as well as government, to multiply taxes, that each by itself might be lighter, and the whole might better reach every class of persons. Governments have therefore multiplied partial taxes. They have taken wherever they have found any thing to take; and though flattering themselves with having thus reached all their subjects, it would be impossible for them to appreciate how much is asked of each class, and consequently to maintain the proportional equality which justice would have required. On the other hand, contributors like better to submit to this heavy inconvenience, than to the obligations of exhibiting an account of their incomes, which, often they do not know themselves, and to a division on arbitrary grounds, which most frequently would be intolerable.

In establishing those different taxes, four rules appear of essential importance for rendering each tax as little burdensome as possible. Each citizen must contribute, if he can do so, according to the proportion of his fortune; the collection must not be expensive, that so the tax may cost as little to the people as possible beyond what it brings into the treasury; the term of payment must be suitable to the contributor, who might frequently be. ruined by an unreasonable demand of what he could pay, without constraint, if his convenience were consulted; and, finally, the citizen's liberty must be respected, that so he may not be exposed otherwise, than with extreme cautions to the inspection of revenue-officers, to the dependent, and all the vexatious measures too often connected with the levying of taxes.

Among the taxes that reach with any equality all classes of contributors, some are proportioned to the income of each, others to the expense of each. These two ways of estimating fortunes seem capable of being adopted indifferently. and, if the expense is not proportionate to the wealth, there is no inconvenience, if the impost, which is regulated by this expense, be, as it were, a bonus on economy, or a fine on prodigality. Tithes, the land-tax, the income-tax, are destined to reach what the contributor receives. Taxes on consumable articles are the chief species of contribution on expenditure. There remains, however, a great number of other taxes, which cannot be arranged under these two heads, and which, accordingly, are not in proportion to the contributor's fortune.

The revenue most easily attained by taxation is that which proceeds from land; because this species of wealth cannot be concealed from sight; because, without the proprietor's declaration, the value of it may be known, and because, in gathering the produce at the moment when nature grants it, we are sure exactly to meet the proprietor's convenience for paying it. But economists are divided in opinion as to the two modes of collecting this tax, the one in kind from the unaltered product, the other in money from the proprietor's net revenue.

Tithes, a tax, according to the first of those methods, is leveled at the moment of abundance, before the producer has in any shape taken possession of his property. The rule, according to which tithes are established, is so universal, that few discussions or vexations arise from it, and this gives it a great appearance of equality. The collection of a tax in kind requires a great number of clerks and warehouses, and hence it is expensive; but this inconvenience might be repaid, if government, after the collection, kept in its granaries the corn delivered to it, till a period more favourable for sale. As cultivators generally cannot wait for this period, the loss suffered by a premature sale would, perhaps, of itself, cover all the charges of collection. Combining such advantages, a national impost in the shape of tithes has seduced many political speculators. Tithes have also been defended with obstinacy by the powerful body to whom they are in general abandoned. Those advantages do not extend to what are called small tithes, an impost vexatious in all its details; the difficult collection of which is an ever fresh root of hatred between the curate and his parishioners, though the impost was intended to unite them all as a single family.

But the advantages of tithes, in any shape, are more than compensated by their real inequality, and the obstacles they oppose to industry. The expense of cultivation is far from being the same in good and in bad soils; in good and bad years; yet the reimbursement of that expense is made by part of the crop, and this part at least should not be subjected to any tax, for fear of destroying the reproduction of the following year. It is not the revenue alone that is tithed; but at the same time all the seed, the manure, the days of labour, which have produced the crop: for all this, the latter ought to restore. In good years, and good soils, two sheaves in ten may represent all these advances: in bad years or soils, eight in ten scarcely cover them; it is not very rare even that the whole crop is insufficient to pay the expenses. Tithes, however, are equally levied in all those cases; from the first they take an eighth part of the land revenue; from the second a half; from the third, which is nothing, they take a portion of the capital destined to produce the following crop; and their inequality is the more cruel, because it is always the poor whom they oppress, taking most from the very persons whose necessity requires most moderation.

Again, the more productive a mode of cultivation is, the more advances does it need to have committed to the ground. Tithes, which are but the seventh or eighth part of the revenue in a pasturage, become the fifth in a field of corn, the third in a vineyard, the half in a hop-yard or in a field of hemp, and the whole in a garden. Thus whilst the national interest incessantly requires the raw produce to be incessantly increased by committing larger advances to the ground-tithes instruct the cultivator incessantly to diminish his advances, and follow that species of culture which gives back least to the nation, but which also least exposes him who undertakes it to be punished for his industry.

The land tax has not the same inconveniences; it affects only the net revenue; it is enabled to reach it with equality enough, and above all, with a regularity which screens the contributor from every arbitrary proceeding, and which, therefore, is to him more precious than justice itself. On being established, it strips the proprietor of a considerable portion of his fortune, for he loses all at once a part of the very capital whose rent alone must pay the tax; but this loss, after having stuck him, is never repeated. From that time he no longer looks upon this capital as belonging to him; a new purchaser, on buying the land, does not pay him any price for this portion; the state has become thenceforth its true proprietor. On the other hand, this territorial impost often requires money from such as have none; it forces them to sell their commodities to obtain the quantity wanted, perhaps at the most unfavourable moment; and it thus contributes to cause a glut in the market at the moment of harvest, and a scarcity at the year's end. Besides, if too heavy, it discourages the proprietor from laying out new advances upon land which he looks upon as scarcely any longer his.

If the capitalist could as easily be come at as the proprietor of land, it would be quite as just to tax him directly for the support of a government which guards his property. The interest of money would be a taxable material, fully as suitable as the rent of land. But the capitalist' s wealth cannot be known without a vexatious inquest, which, in trading counties, would be destructive to credit. Capitals, moreover, are not attached to the soil, and if loaded with imposts, the capitalist would be induced to transmit them into other counties, often without emigrating himself. He would thus deprive his country of all the labour which those capitals would support; he would diminish the national revenues in a proportion immensely superior to the advantages which the treasury could expect from the new tax.

Other species of revenue escape still more easily from direct contribution. A considerable revenue in the state, for example, is the profit of trade and that of manufacture; but, on being directly taxed, it is almost sure to be annihilated. Another very considerable revenue is that of workmen, who gain but a mere wage; the great number of those who enjoy it, makes up for the slenderness of the portion belonging to each. Such also are the revenues of all those classes whose labours leave no products which are substantial and capable of accumulation. Most men who live by those different means, do not even know the extent of their revenue; because, receiving it day by day, and expending it in the same manner, they think they have nothing when their labour is all that remains. They form the poorest class of society, but also the most numerous; and, if we add up the annual consumption of all the day-labourers, it is greatly superior in value to that of all the rich.

But before we think of taxing this revenue, we must remember, that nothing can be more absurd, as well as cruel, than to take away a part of the necessary emolument of productive workmen; for, either it must actually be paid by them, in which case they would suffer, languish, and at last die of penury, and with them would also be destroyed the national revenue, which should spring from their labour; or else they would succeed in obtaining reimbursement for their contribution, either on the class which employs them, or on that of consumers. F or this purpose, they would raise either all their wages, or the price of all their produce. Thus they would raise manufactures, or, at least, shut foreign markets; and, by a circuit a little longer, they would equally arrest production, and destroy the national revenue. No operation, however, could be more difficult than to separate, in a poor man's revenue, the necessary from the superfluous, which alone can be taxed. Besides, such a tax would be to fix contribution on labour and industry; or, in some degree, to inflict a penalty on those qualities which it is the most essential to encourage; it would be to arrest, at their source, the wealth and prosperity of states. Such are the motives which have generally prevented a universal tax on income; or, at least, have prevented it from reaching the industrious classes completely enough to become productive.

But those different kinds of income, which cannot be appreciated for taxation, at their origin, are always employed in consumption; and this is the moment when taxation can reach them with far less inconvenience. By taxing every kind of goods, in the purchasing of which wealth may be employed, we are sure to make that wealth contribute, and we need not know to whom it belongs. For such a contribution there is not required any declaration of fortune, any inquisition, any distinction of poor and rich; it does not attach taxation to labour; it does not punish what ought, above all other things, to be encouraged. Besides, each contributor pays his taxes on consumption, as it were in a voluntary manner, at the time when he has money, and finds himself enabled to purchase the thing taxed; he reimburses the merchant, who has already advanced the impost, and he scarcely perceives that himself has paid any.

Taxes on consumption are, however, very far from being able to reach the revenue in a correct manner, by means of the expenditure. It is required, for example, that every kind of fortune, every kind of industry, protected by the state, should pay the treasury ten per cent. of the revenue which they give. At first view it appears that this object would be obtained by taxing every consumption, every expense, of what nature soever, at ten per cent. of its value. But if we attempt to come at every kind of consumption, we must subject to the same tax the commodities produced in the interior of families by domestic industry, those produced by the national manufactures, and those introduced by foreign commerce. By making exceptions to this rule, not only would the principle of equality he destroyed, in a very unjust manner, but also each would be induced to serve himself, greatly to the prejudice of manufactures, trade, and the division of labour, which much increases its productive power. On the other hand, by following it rigorously out, each family would be subjected to an inspection of its domestic economy, absolutely insupportable.

The universality of such a tax would have a still more fatal inconvenience, if it were extended to commodities of prime necessity. By exempting such commodities, a very considerable portion of the national expenditure is left out; but, in taxing them, the risk is run of confounding the necessary with the superfluous, in the poor man's consumption; and, should the former be encroached on, of arresting the reproduction of revenue, either by the penury and death of the workman, or by the rising of his wages.

In the last place, no idea could be entertained of taxing goods destined for exportation; because, whenever the price of them was raised, foreign consumers would provide themselves elsewhere; it would be necessary, in that case, to restore, by drawbacks, all the customs levied on them. But how could endless frauds upon this principle be avoided? The vexatious laws intended to subject foreign commerce to a constant superintendence, to prevent such frauds, would alone be equivalent to a heavy contribution.

It is a great inconvenience of taxes on consumption, that

it never can be known at their establishment who is to pay them in the long run. The legislature always proposes to make them be reimbursed by the consumer; but sometimes they do not reach his distance; at other times, they do not stop at him, and the consumer is anew reimbursed for them by those for whom he labours. To make the consumer pay the whole tax, the nation must be in a state of increasing prosperity; for otherwise, as the consumer is not richer than before the tax, he cannot devote more money than formerly to his enjoyments, and must, therefore, in some shape, diminish his consumption. The producer, on his side, no longer selling the whole of his goods, must diminish his production, or consent to pay a portion of the tax. If a public calamity happens, a scarcity or even a state of embarrassment in trade, consumption still further diminishes; and the producer, compelled to dispose of his goods, pays the whole tax; till, no longer finding any profit in his labour, he abandons it entirely.

On the other hand, when taxes and consumption have raised the price of every thing, industrious men, who form a numerous class among consumers, no longer find in their industry sufficient resources to support them. His wages no longer furnish the day-labourer with those limited enjoyments which are to be reckoned among the necessaries of life, since life, or the power of labouring, could not long be maintained in an individual deprived of every pleasure. He struggles, therefore, with all his strength, to get his wages increased; the manufacturer and merchant, in like manner, to get their profits increased. As the total sale diminishes, it is necessary for their subsistence that they obtain more for each separate article. Their joint efforts soon succeed in raising the price of all goods coming from their hands, but especially goods of prime necessity, because the sellers of these give the law to buyers, who cannot do without such goods. A rise in the price of those commodities reacts anew on wages and profits; the disorganisation becomes complete; national productions cost much higher than those of countries not oppressed by a similar system; they cannot support a competition in foreign markets; exportation ceases, demand is not renewed, and the nation sinks under a frightful distress.

If a universal impost on consumption presents insuperable difficulties, partial imposts are equally liable to inconveniences. When one kind of goods has been taxed by universal custom, as salt is, a considerable sum of money has indeed been raised; but a tax on consumption has been changed into a sort of capitation, which weighs equally upon the poor and upon the rich, without any regard to the contributor's fortune, or his means of making payment. The salt tax, when so considerable that the day-labourer feels the weight of it, is, perhaps, the most unequal of all imposts. The poorest house consumes as much as the richest; but the poor must take, from what is essentially necessary to their subsistence, a sum which the rich scarcely notice in their superfluity.

It were vain to seek, among articles of consumption, for one which is proportioned to expenditure or to wealth; some are sought after by the rich alone, hut they do not use them in proportion to their riches. A duty of consumption on tea, sugar, spices, does not reach a class so numerous as a duty on salt; but among those paying it, this duty is proportioned only to what a single individual can employ in his use. It spares the poor, but it weighs not upon the rich; it is, consequently, very unproductive, whilst duties extending to the smallest consumption are the only ones which bring in much to government.

By degrees, duties on consumption have been extended to every kind of production. It has been imagined that if the rich man was made to pay a first capitation on salt, a second on light, a third on drink, a fourth on food, a fifth on clothes, there would be established a kind of proportion between his contributions and his fortune; because he would pay a much greater number of taxes than the poor man, although each tax, being limited by the individual's physical wants, was disproportioned to his wealth. The impossibility of establishing a uniform and universal law, was clearly felt; and the attempt was made of approximating to it, by a multitude of partial laws.

Hence has arisen a fourfold division of duties on consumption, which are adopted in almost all countries; namely, the gabelle, custom, excise, and tolls. The gabelle comprises those commodities of which the government claims a monopoly, salt and tobacco, for example; it sells them alone, at a high price, by its agents or favourites, and prosecutes by rigorous penalties all such as attempt to take a share in their manufacture or trade. Customs are destined to levy a proportionate duty on goods imported from foreign counties; and the excise, or aids on goods produced in the country itself. The former is only established in the confines of the territory; and although the advancement in price of those taxed commodities is equally felt over the whole state, the vexations which accompany the levying of duties are confined to the frontiers alone. The latter is to levy the tax wherever industry is exercised; it consequently must comprehend, under its inspection, all productive workmen, all the most useful citizens of the state; and it cannot reach them, except by an inquisition almost constantly destructive of security and freedom. Tolls, in the last place, established at the gates of towns, form the fourth class of duties on consumption. As the most important department of the national exchange is that between the industry of towns and the industry of the country, tolls are destined to reach the latter, and to subject the goods produced by agriculture to a proportionate tax, at the moment when they come to be consumed by the inhabitants of towns.

In this manner, the establishment of taxes on consumption has covered Europe with four hosts of clerks, inspectors, agents, who, by incessantly struggling with each citizen about pecuniary interests, have contributed to render authority odious to the people, and accustomed men to elude the law, to violate truth, to disobey, and to deceive. The more heavy and multiplied these taxes are, the more rapidly will immorality make progress. Goods destined for the consumption of the rich, presenting, in the same bulk, a much greater value than goods consumed by the poor, offer a much more powerful encouragement to smuggling; they have hence been necessarily subjected to far lower duties, that fraud might not altogether escape with them from taxation; and by pushing things to extremes, the most unjust inequality has been established among contributors; liberty has been encroached on by vexatious inquisitions; the manufactures, the trade, even the existence of those who labour and who should create every kind of wealth, have been endangered. Those counties which have enjoyed the highest prosperity are exactly those in which this aggravation of indirect taxes threatens every kind of industry with the most complete ruin.

Governments have not been contented with taxing revenues and expenditure; they have gone forth to seek out all the acts of civil life which might afford them an opportunity of asking money. Some have established capitations, which, weighing equally on the poor and the rich, force the man to pay who has nothing, for whom society does nothing, equally with him who has too much; for whom society lays out enormous expenses. Others have attacked with considerable imposts, inheritances, sales, and all exchange of property; though, in thus encroaching on capital, not on revenue, they diminish the productive cause of wealth, nearly as if tithes were levied on the seed, instead of being levied on the crop. Others have established imposts on loans, by pledge and judicial acts, on stamps, and a train of accidents which ought to be taken as Symptoms of poverty, not of riches. Others, in fine, by establishing lotteries, have profited by encouraging a ruinous vice.

This review of the different kinds of taxation shows clearly, that one of the most essential qualities which a nation can ask in its government is economy. States, in the vigour lent them by freedom, in the full enjoyment of all their advantages, give way to all the dreams of ambition; they listen to all the suggestions of pride, of jealousy, or of vengeance; under the pretext of being on their guard against distant or imaginary dangers, they rush headlong, with light hearts, into ruinous wars, and persist in them with obstinacy; though the voice of humanity calls for peace in vain, the superiority of their nation does not yet appear sufficiently established, their enemy is not yet sufficiently humbled; the work which they thought accomplished has been overturned; it must be reestablished at any price. Present resources, however, are exhausted, and recourse is had to borrowing: credit is still entire; the national capitals are drained away from commerce, and placed, one after another, at the disposal of a minister, who dissipates them, and replaces them by assignments on the future; and the passion which blinded men for a few months, condemns their posterity to suffering for ages.

Perhaps no invention was ever more fatal to men than that of public loans: none is yet enveloped with more illusions. The passions excited by politics are so violent; the questions to be decided by negotiations or by arms so important; all sacrifices become so natural, when the prosperity, the existence, the honour of all are at stake, that governments and the people, before yielding, are to exhaust every resource to the very uttermost. They will send out the last man to battle, they will expend their last shilling, if they can possibly dispose of either; and they will do this not alone for the safety of the people, but for any war, any quarrel in which they happen to engage, because there is no one in which their offended pride may not be confounded with honour, in which they cannot honestly say what is true only in extreme cases, that a nation had better cease to exist than exist dishonoured.

If the possibility of making such preternatural exertions could be furnished to nations, and reserved at the same time for an extraordinary necessity, no doubt a great service would be done to human society, which is shaken to its foundation every time that one of its members is overthrown. But each mean of defence becomes in its turn a mean of attack. The invention of artillery, happy for society if it could have been employed only in the defence of towns, has served to overthrow them: the invention of standing armies has opposed discipline to discipline, and talent to talent; the invention of conscriptions has opposed all the youth of one nation to all the youth of another; the invention of landsthurms and levees en masse, has made even women and old men descend to the field of battle to assist regular troops; the invention of loans has attacked and defended the present generation, with all the hope and all the labour of posterity. The strength of nations, though becoming still more formidable, has continued still in same proportion. The state, in danger, has not found deliverance more easily. but humanity herself has been sacrificed, and, amid those gigantic combats, it is she that must perish.

As, after those destructive expenses rendered possible by loans, there remains an apparent wealth, which has been named the public funds, and which figures as an immense capital, the different portions of which constitute the fortunes of opulent individuals, some have believed, or affected to believe, that this dissipation of national capital was not so great an evil, but rather a circulation, which caused wealth to spring up again under another shape; and that mysterious advantages existed for great states in this immaterial opulence, which was seen to pass from hand to hand on the market of the public stocks.

No very powerful logic was needed, to persuade ministers of the advantages arising from dissipation; stock-jobbers, of the national profit attached to their commerce; state creditors, of the importance of their rank in society; capitalists, eager to lend, of the service they did to the public, by taking from it an interest superior to that of trade. Thus all appeared amply satisfied with regard to the unintelligible doctrine by which it was pretended to demonstrate the advantage of public funds.

In place of following this subtle reasoning, we shall endeavour to show that stocks are nothing else but the imaginary capital, which represents that portion of the annual revenue set apart for paying the debt. An equivalent capital has been dissipated; it is this which gives name to the loan; but it is not this which stocks represent, for this does not any where exist. New wealth, however, must spring from labour and industry. A yearly portion of this wealth is assigned beforehand to those who have lent the wealth already destroyed; the loan will abstract this portion from its producer, to bestow it on the state creditor, according to the proportion between capital and interest usual in the country: and an imaginary capital is conceived to exist, equivalent to what would yield the annual revenue which the creditors are to receive.

As, in lending to a merchant or a landed proprietor, we acquire a right to part of the revenue which arises from the merchant's trade, or from the proprietor's land, but diminish their revenue by the precise sum which increases our own; so in lending to government we acquire a right to that part of the merchant's or proprietor's revenue, which government will seize by taxation to pay us. We are enriched only as contributors are impoverished. Private and public credit are a part of individual, but not of national wealth; for nothing is wealth but what gives a revenue, and credit gives none to the nation. If all public and private debts were abolished in a day, there would be a frightful overturning of property. one family would be ruined for the profit of another, but the nation would neither be richer nor poorer, and the one party would have gained what the other had lost. This has not, however, in any case, been the result of public bankruptcies; because governments, whilst suppressing their debts, have maintained the taxation which belonged to their creditors; or rather they have broken their faith to the latter, and have continued notwithstanding to encroach on the property of contributors.

A government which borrows, after leaving dissipated its capital, makes posterity perpetually debtor in the clearest part of the profit arising from its work. An overwhelming burden is cast upon it, to bow down, one generation after another. Public calamities may occur, trade may take a new direction, rivals may supplant us. The reproduction which is sold beforehand may never reappear; yet not withstanding we are loaded with a debt above our strength, with a debt of hypothecating our future labour, which we shall not perhaps be able to accomplish.

The necessity of paying this debt begets oppressive imposts of one kind or another; all become equally fatal when too much multiplied. They overwhelm industry, and destroy that reproduction which is already sold beforehand. The more that it has paid already, the less capable does the nation become of paying farther. One part of the revenue was to spring from agriculture - but taxation has ruined agriculture; another proceeded from manufactures, but taxation has closed up those establishments; another yet from trade, but taxation has banished trade. The suffering continues to increase, all the resources to diminish. The moment arrives at last, when a frightful bankruptcy becomes inevitable. And doubts are entertained whether it should not even be hastened, that the salvation of the state may yet be attempted. There remains no chance to shield the whole subjects of the state from ruin; but if the creditors are allowed to perish first, perhaps the debtors will escape; if the debtors perish from penury, with them will be extinguished the last hope of the creditors, who must soon perish in their turn.

Chapter 7: Of Population

We have defined political economy, as being the investigation of the means, by which the greatest number of men in a given state may participate in the highest degree of physical happiness, so far as it depends on government. Two elements, indeed, must always be received in connexion by the legislature; the increase of happiness in intensity, and the diffusion of it among all classes of subjects. It is thus that political economy, on a great scale, becomes the theory of beneficence; and that every thing which does not in the long run concern the happiness of men belongs not to this science.

The human race originating in a single family, has multiplied, and spread itself by degrees over the globe; and much time was of course required, before it could be adjusted to the means of subsistence, which different parts of this globe are capable of supplying. We see this work of nature repeated in new counties, or in a colony established in a desert region. A state which passes from barbarism to a higher stage of civilization, cannot all on a sudden become covered with as many inhabitants as it may comfortably support: as the earth has been wasted several times; as the greater part of its provinces has been by turns plunged into a state of desolation, to arise from it slowly afterwards, we have often had the opportunity of witnessing this spectacle of a growing population. We are accustomed to consider it as the mark of prosperity and good government; and hence our law and constitution all tend to favour this increase, though to increase the symptoms of prosperity is very different from increasing prosperity itself.

Nature has attended to the multiplication of races with a kind of profusion. Although that of man is among the slowest in its progress, it may increase, when all circumstances are favourable, far more quickly than any of our observations indicate. When every man has a great interest in bringing up a family, and has the means of doing so; when all marry, and all as young as nature permits; when they continue to have children till the approaches of old age, their posterity increases so as very quickly to occupy all the allotted space. In several counties, in consequence of the social organization, not above a fourth part of the individuals marry; the rest grow old in celibacy. Yet this fourth is of itself sufficient to keep up the population at the same level. If their brothers and sisters could also marry with the same advantage, the population would be quadrupled in a single generation.

Thus, every nation very soon arrives at the degree of population which it can attain without changing its social institutions. It soon arrives at counting as many individuals as it can maintain with a revenue so limited, and so distributed. If a great transient calamity, a war, a pestilence, a famine, have left a great void in the population, should those events be followed by a period of general security and comfort, this renewing power of human generation is speedily developed; and an observer is astonished to see how few years are required to obliterate all traces of a scourge, which seemed to have unpeopled the earth. But, on the other hand, so soon as this term has been reached, a greater increase of the population is a national calamity; the earth soon consumes those whom it cannot feed. The more numerous births are, the more will mortality display its ravages, to maintain constantly the same level; and this mortality, the effect of misery and suffering, is preceded by the lengthened punishments not of those who perish only, but of those who have struggled with them for existence.

In every country, it is essential to know well those different periods of increase, of stagnation and decline, in order to adapt the laws, and all social institutions, to the circumstances; and not, as has too frequently been done, to hasten, with all our efforts, the destruction we ought most to fear.

So long as a great part of the country is uncultivated as land proper for liberally rewarding rural labour is covered only with spontaneous production; as even the part under tillage is imperfectly worked; as the soil is not rendered healthy, the marshes drained, the hills protected against precipitations, the fields defended against the ruinous force of nature; so long as all this is not done merely for want of hands - it is desirable for the happiness of agriculturists, and for that of the nation living on their labour, that the class of cultivators should be increased, and enabled to accomplish the task reserved for them.

So long as the objects produced by the industrious arts are imperfectly supplied to the consumer, or at least as he cannot procure them except by a sacrifice quite disproportionate to their value; so long as he is constrained to furnish himself coarsely by domestic industry, for want of opportunity to buy furniture, effects, clothes, proper for his use; so long as his enjoyments are restricted by the inconveniences of all the utensils with which he is obliged to content himself, - it is desirable that the manufacturing population increase; since, from the need there is of such a population, it might evidently live in comfort, and contribute to the enjoyment of other classes.

So long as all hands are in such a degree necessary for agriculture, and manufactures, or trade which serves them, that the guardian professions, equally useful to society, are badly filled up - it is desirable that population continue to increase, that so interior order, security of person and property, may be better protected, health better attended to, the soul better nourished, the mind more enlightened; and that society may be externally defended with sufficient force, comprehending even the rapid recruitment of a sea or land army, which consume population.

This population, indeed, whenever it is required, will quickly be replaced. But it is not enough that it be replaced, if it cannot find the niche, to which it is destined. Sometimes a fertile soil is in vain abundant, and remains uncultivated. There is no chance of the most numerous population assembled in its neighbourhood coming to profit by its resources. This soil has become the property of a few families; it is declared indivisible and unalienable; it will always pass to a single proprietor, according to the order of primogeniture, without the capacity either to be subjected to an emphyteutic lease, or burdened with a mortgage. The proprietor has not the capital necessary for its cultivation; he can give no security to such as have this capital, that will engage them to employ it in his land. Thus the idle population of Rome in vain calls for labour; the waste Campagna di Roma in vain calls for labourers; the social organization is bad; and so long as this shall remain unchanged, the day-labourer will perish from penury, on the surface of fields which, for want of culture, are returning to their wild state; and the population, far from increasing, will diminish.

On the same principle in manufactures, the rich proprietors of Poland will in vain require all the produce of luxury; the bad condition of the roads, prohibiting every distant transport, will in vain present superior advantages to national industry; oppression and servitude destroy all energy, all spirit of enterprise in the lower class. Elsewhere ruinous monopolies, absurd privileges, affrighting advances, ignorance, barbarity, and want of security, will render the progress of manufactures impossible; no capital will be accumulated to animate them. In those cases, to increase the population will not increase industry. The births will in vain be doubled, be quadrupled, during a certain number of years; they will not afford an additional workman, they will only be followed by a proportionably quicker mortality. The social organization is bad; so long as this shall remain unchanged, population cannot increase.

The guardian population is fed as well as recruited by the other classes. It is not sufficient that many children are born; unless their parents enjoy a certain degree of opulence, they can never bring them up to the age of men; the prince can never make soldiers of them. In this case, wars by land or sea will devour the population; whilst they employ only its superfluity, the social organization is good.

The population is always measured, in the long run, by the demand for labour. Wherever labour is required, and a sufficient wage offered, the workmen will arise to earn it. The population, with its expansive force, will occupy the place which is found vacant. Subsistence will also arise for the workmen, or in case of need, be imported. The same demand which calls a man into existence, will likeWise recompense the agricultural labour which provides him with food. If the demand for labour cease, the workman will perish, yet not without a struggle, in which not he alone will suffer, but all his brethren and his rivals. The subsistence which enabled him to live, and which henceforth he cannot pay for, and cannot demand, will, in its turn, cease to be produced. Thus national happiness rests on the demand for labour, but on a regular and perpetual demand. For, on the contrary, a demand which is intermittent, after having formed workmen, condemns them to suffering and death: it would be far better if they never had existed.

We have seen that the demand for labour, the cause of production, must be proportional to revenue which supports consumption; that this revenue, in its turn, originates in the national wealth, which wealth is formed and augmented by labour. Thus, in political economy, all things are linked together, we move constantly in a circle; since each effect becomes a cause in its turn. Yet all things are progressive, provided that each movement is adjusted to the rest; but all stops, all retrogrades, whenever one of the movements which ought to be combined is disordered. According to the natural march of things, an augmentation of wealth will produce an augmentation of revenue; from this will arise an increase of consumption, next an increase of labour for reproduction, and therewith of population; and, finally, this new labour will, in its turn, increase the national wealth. But if, by unreasonable measures, any one of those operations is hastened without regard to all the rest, the whole system is deranged, and the poor are weighed down with suffering, instead of the happiness which was

123

anticipated for them.

The object of society is not fulfilled, so long as the country occupied by this society, presents means of supporting a new population, of enabling it to live in happiness and abundance, whilst yet those means are not resorted to. The multiplication of happiness over the earth, is the object of Providence; it is stamped in all his works, and the duty of men in their human society is to co-operate in it.

The government which, by oppression of its subjects, by its contempt for justice and order, by the shackles it puts on agriculture and industry, condemns fertile counties to be deserts, sins not against its own subjects alone; its tyranny is a crime against human society, on the whole of which it inflicts suffering; it weakens its rights over the country occupied by it, and as it troubles the enjoyments of all other states, it gives to all others the right of controlling it. All men are mutually necessary to each other. Europe has a double need of the subsistence which it might procure from Barbary, if this magnificent shore of Africa were given back to civilization, and from the consumers we should soon find there. The institution of property is the result of social conventions. In a society subjected to laws and a regulating government, the interest of each may be implicitly relied on for producing the advantage of all, because the aberrations of this private interest are, in every case of need, limited by public authority. But, in the great human society formed among independent nations, there is no law or general government to repress the passions of each sovereign: besides, the interest of those sovereigns is not necessarily conformable to that of their subjects; or, to speak more correctly, the one is contrary to the other, whenever the object of the rulers is to maintain their tyranny. Thus respect for the pretended right of properly claimed by each government over its territory, is not referrible to the right of private property, and, besides, it cannot be reciprocal. The same circumstances which cause a tyrannical government to impede its own civilization, render it equally incapable of respecting that of its neighbours, and submitting to the laws of nations.

But whilst more than three quarters of the habitable globe are, by the faults of their governments, deprived of the inhabitants they should support, we, at the present day, in almost the whole of Europe, experience the opposite calamity, that of not being able to maintain a superabundant population, which surpasses the proportion of labour required, and which, before dying of poverty, will diffuse its sufferings over the whole class of such as live by the labour of their hands. For our part, we owe this calamity to the imprudent zeal of our governments. With us, religious instruction, legislation, social organization, every thing has tended to produce a population, the existence of which was not provided for beforehand. The labour was not adjusted to the number of men; and, frequently, the same zeal with which it was attempted to multiply the number of births, was afterwards employed, in all arts, to diminish the required number of hands. The proportion which should subsist in the progress of the different departments of society has been broken, and the suffering has become universal.

Mr Malthus, the first writer who awakened public attention to this calamity under which nations have long suffered, without knowing it, whilst he gave an alarm to legislators, did not reach the true principles which he seemed on the road to find. On reading his writings, one is stuck at once with an essential error in his reasoning, and with the importance of the facts to which he appeals. Such confusion, in a matter to which the happiness of man is attached, may produce the most fatal consequences. By rigorously applying principles deficient in accuracy, the most grievous errors may be committed; and if, on the other hand, the error is discovered, there is a risk of simultaneously rejecting both the observations and the precepts.

Mr Malthus established as a principle that the population of every country is limited by the quantity of subsistence which that country can furnish. This proposition is true only when applied to the whole terrestial globe, or to a country which has no possibility of trade; in all other cases, foreign trade modifies it; and, farther, which is more important, this proposition is but abstractly true, - true in a manner inapplicable to political economy. Population has never reached the limit of subsistence, and probably it never will. Long before the population can be arrested by the inability of the country to produce more food, it is arrested by the inability of the population to purchase that food, or to labour in producing it.

The whole population of a state, says Mr Malthus, may be doubled every twenty-five years; it would thus follow a geometrical progression: but the labour employed to meliorate a soil, already in culture, can add to its produce nothing but quantities continually decreasing. Admitting that, during the first twenty-five years, the produce of land has been doubled, during the second we shall scarcely succeed in compelling it to produce a half more, then a third more, then a fourth. Thus the progress of subsistence will not follow the geometrical, but the arithmetical progression; and, in the course of two centuries, whilst the population increases, as the numbers, 1. 2, 4, 8, 16, 32, 64, 128, subsistence will increase not faster than the numbers, 1, 2, 3, 4, 5, 6, 7, 8.

This reasoning, which serves as a basis to the system of Mr. Malthus, and to which he incessantly appeals, through the whole course of his book, is completely sophistical. It opposes the possible increase of the human population, considered abstractly, and without regarding circumstances, to the positive increase of animals and vegetables in a confined place, under circumstances more and more unfavourable. They ought not thus to be compared. Abstractly, the multiplication of food follows a geometrical progression, no less than the multiplication of men. It follows it only in a much more rapid manner. In a given space and time, this progression is not followed any more by the one species than the other. Population is arrested first, and arrests subsistence in its turn; when the obstacle is removed, both begin again to increase, till they reach a new limit, equally common to both; and the history of the universe has never yet presented the example of a country in which the multiplication of food could not be more rapid than that of the co-existent population.

In a state absolutely savage, men live on the produce of hunting and fishing. The fish and the game are multiplied like man, in a geometrical progression, but much more rapid than the one he follows. Man, it is true, hinders their reproduction by destroying them; but, on the other hand, they arrest his; for it is not certainly among nations of hunters that the population is doubled every twenty-five years; and whenever this destruction is suspended, the reproduction of game will be much more rapid than that of men.

The progress of civilization substitutes the pastoral life for a life of hunting; and the natural produce of the ground, better managed, is sufficient for a much more numerous population of men and of animals. The deserts, which scarcely support five hundred Cherokee hunters, would be sufficient for ten thousand Tartar shepherds, with all their flocks; the multiplication of the latter is always much more rapid than that of men; whilst the production of a man requires twenty-five years, that of an ox requires but five, of a sheep but two, of a hog but one. The number of oxen may be doubled in six years, that of sheep in three, that of hogs may be rendered ten times as great in two years. Whenever a shepherd gains possession of a country formerly abandoned to hunting, the multiplication of his flocks will greatly precede that of his family; when, afterwards, one of the two is arrested, the other will be so too.

But when civilization makes a new step, pastoral nations abandon their flocks for agriculture; and, instead of trusting to the natural productions of the vegetable kingdom, they produce and multiply them by their labours. It is calculated that thirty families may live on the corn produced by a piece of ground, which would have supported only a single family by its produce in cattle. At the time, therefore, when a nation passes from the pastoral to the agricultural state, it in some sense acquires a country thirty times as large as the one it formerly occupied. If the whole of this country is not cultivated, if even in the most civilized kingdoms, there remains a vast extent nf fertile land still employed in unprofitable pasturage, it is an evident proof that other causes than want of subsistence prevent the development of population.

The multiplication of vegetables follows a geometrical progression much more rapid still than the multiplication of cattle. In common tillage, corn increases five-fold in the course of a year; potatoes ten-fold in the same space of time. The latter vegetable, to produce a given quantity of food, scarcely requires the tenth part of the ground which corn would occupy. Yet even in the most populous countries, men are very far from having planted all their corn fields with potatoes; from having sown all their pasturages with corn; from having converted into pasturage all their woods, all their deserts abandoned to hunting. Those things are a fund of reserve remaining to every nation; and, by means of them, if a new demand for labour should suddenly cause the population to increase as rapidly as the nature of man can permit, the multiplication of food would still precede it.

The demand for labour which the capital of a country can pay, and not the quantity of food which that country can produce, regulates the population. In political economy, nothing is reckoned a demand but what is accompanied with a sufficient compensation for the thing demanded. If no fault has been committed on the part of government, if no dangerous prejudice has been diffused among the people, very few men will think of marrying, and burdening their hands with the subsistence of individuals unable to procure it themselves, till they have first acquired an establishment. But whenever a new demand for labour raises their wages, and thus increases their revenue, they hasten to satisfy one of the first laws of nature, and seek in marriage a new source of happiness. If the rise of wages was but momentary; if, for example, the favours granted by government suddenly give a great development to a species of manufacture, which, after its commencement, cannot be maintained, the workmen, whose remuneration was double during some time, will all have married to profit by their opulence; and then, at the moment when their trade declines, families disproportionate to the actual demand of labour will be plunged into the most dreadful wretchedness.

It is those variations in the demand for labour, this sort of revolution so frequent in the lives of poor artisans, that gives to the state a superabundant population. Already brought into the world, that population finds no longer any room to exist there; it is always ready to be satisfied with the lowest terms on which it may be permitted to live. There is no condition so hard that men are not found ready to engage in it voluntarily. In some trades, the workmen are obliged to live in mud, exposed to continual nausea; in others, the labour engenders painful and inevitable maladies; several stupify the senses, degrade the body and the soul; several employ none but children, and after introducing into life, abandon to a horrible indigence the being they have formed. There are callings, in fine, which public opinion brands with infamy; there are some which deserve this condemnation. Yet the ranks are always full; and a miserable wage, scarce sufficient for existence, induces men, to undergo so many evils. The reason is, society does not leave them any choice; they are compelled to be contented with this cruel lot or not to live. The duty of governments to succour so much wretchedness cannot be doubtful, for they are almost always the cause of this wretched population's being created; but, at the same time they ought not to forget that it is their part to save from indigence the miserable creatures already in existence, though at the same time discouraging them from perpetuating their race. Assistance given to the poor has often done the contrary.

Religious instruction has almost always strongly contributed to destroy the equilibrium between the population, and the demand for labour which is to give it subsistence. When questions of moral polity are introduced in a religious system, it almost constantly happens, that the cause of the precept is absolutely separated from the precept itself; and a rule, which should be modified by circumstances, becomes an invariable law. Religions began with the origin of the human race; and therefore at a time when the rapid progress of population was every where desirable; their principles have not yet changed, now when the unlimited increase of families has given birth only to beings, of necessity condemned to physical suffering or moral degradation.

A Chinese knows no greater misfortune, no deeper humiliation, than not to leave sons behind him to perform the funeral honours at his death. In almost all other creeds the indefinite increase of families has ever been represented as a blessing of heaven. On the other hand, whilst religion repressed irregularity of morals, it attached all morality of conduct to marriage, and washed away, by the nuptial benediction alone, whatever, was reprehensible in the imprudence of him who inconsiderately contracted the bonds of paternity. Yet, how important soever purity of morals may be, the duties of a father towards those whom he brings into existence are of a still higher order. Children born but for wretchedness, are also born but for vice. The happiness and the virtue of innocent and defenceless beings are thus sacrificed beforehand, to satisfy the passions of a day. The ardour of casuists in preaching up marriage to correct a fault; the imprudence with which they recommend husbands to shut their eyes upon the future, to entrust the fate of their children to providence; the ignorance of social order, which has induced them to erase chastity from the number of virtues proper in marriage, are causes which have been incessantly active in destroying the proportion which naturally would have established itself between the population and its means of existing.

The Catholic faith has sometimes gained credit for its religious vows; which by forbidding marriage to a certain number of individuals, seemed to offer some opposition to an unlimited multiplication of the human species. But those who consider it thus, certainly do not understand another very important part of the legislation of casuists, with regard to all that they have named the duties of husbands. Considering marriage as solely destined for multiplication, they have made a sin of the very virtues which they enforce on single persons. This morality is enforced by every confessor on every father and mother of a family. The effects of it are powerfully felt in the social organization of Catholic countries. They are met with even in reformed churches.

When fatal prejudices are not honoured; when a system of morality contrary to our true duties towards others, and above all towards those indebted to us for life, is not taught in the name of the most sacred authority, no wise man will marry till he is in a condition that affords him sure means of living, no father of a family will have more children than he can conveniently maintain. The latter expects that his children will be satisfied with the lot in which he has lived; hence he will wish the rising generation exactly to represent that which is departing; he will wish that a son and a daughter arrived at the age of marriage, should fill the place of his father and his mother; that his children's children should fill his place and his wife's, in their turn; his daughter will find in another house exactly the lot which he will give to the daughter of another house in his own; and the income which satisfied the fathers will satisfy the children.

When once this family is formed, justice and humanity require that they submit to the same constraints which single people undergo. On considering how small is the number of natural children in every country, it ought to be admitted that this constraint is sufficiently effectual. In a country where population cannot increase, where new places do not exist for new establishments, the father who has eight children should reckon either that six of his children will die young, or that three contemporary males and their contemporary females; or in the following generation three of his sons and three of his daughters

131

will not marry on his account. There is no less injustice in the second calculation than cruelty in the first. If marriage is sacred; if it is one great means of attaching men to virtue, and recompensing the chagrins of declining years, by the growing hopes of allowing an honourable old age to succeed an active youth, it is not because this institution renders lawful the pleasures of sense, but because it imposes new duties on the father of a family, and returns him the sweetest recompense in the ties of husband and father. Religious morality ought therefore to teach men, that marriage is made for all citizens equally; that it is the object towards which they should all direct their efforts; but that this object has not been attained except so far as they are able to fulfil their duties towards the beings whom they call into existence: and after obtaining the happiness of being fathers, after renewing their families, and giving this stay and hope to their declining years, they are no less obliged to live chastely with their wives, than single persons with such as do not belong to them.

Self-interest powerfully warns men against this indefinite multiplication of their families, to which they have been invited by so fatal a religious error, and no one ought to be disquieted if this order is observed remissly. In general at least three births are required to give two such individuals as arrive at the age of marriage; and the niches of population are not so exactly formed, that they cannot by turns admit a little more and a little less. Only government ought to awaken the prudence of citizens deficient in it, and never to deceive them by hopes of an independent lot, when this illusory establishment shall leave them exposed to misery, suffering, and death.

When peasants are proprietors, the agricultural population stops of itself, when it has brought about a division of the land, such that each family is invited to labour, and may live in comfortable circumstances. This is the case in almost all the Swiss cantons, which follow nothing but agriculture. When two or more sons are found in one family, the younger do not marry till they can find wives who bring them some property.

Till then, they work day-labour and live by means of it. But among peasant-cultivators, the trade of day-labour does not afford a rank; and the workman who has nothing but his limbs, can rarely find a father imprudent enough to give him his daughter.

When the land, instead of being cultivated by its proprietors, is cultivated by farmers, metayers, day-labourers, the condition of the latter classes becomes more precarious, and their multiplication is not so necessarily adjusted to the demand for their labour. They are far worse informed than the peasant-proprietor, and yet they are called to perform a much more complicated calculation. Living under the risk of being dismissed at a day' s notice from the land they till, it is less a question with them what this land will give, than what is their chance of being employed elsewhere. They calculate probabilities in place of certainties, and commit themselves to fortune with regard to what they cannot investigate. They depend on being happy; they marry much younger; they bring into the world many more children, precisely because they know less distinctly how those children are to be established.

Thus metayers, day-labourers. all peasants depending on a master, being more imperfectly able to judge of their situation by themselves, ought to be guided and protected by government. Landed proprietors wield all the force of monopoly against them; whilst day-labourers, acting in competition with each other, are finally reduced to work for the most wretched subsistence. Those measures are wise, therefore, which have been adopted by legislators to fix the minimum share that should fall to each peasant. It would, in general, be a beneficent law which should permit no division of a metairie below a certain limit, no reduction below a half on the metayer's part. It is a beneficent law which has fixed the peasant's lot in Austria; a law which should invariably fix the Russian peasant's capitation to his landlord, would be equivalent to an emancipation from serfage, and free from all the convulsions of such a step. The Russian nation could not, perhaps, receive a greater benefit from its government. The statute of Elizabeth, in fine, was wise in prohibiting a cottage from being built without at least four acres of land being allotted to it. Had this law been executed in England and Ireland, no marriage could have happened among day-labourers without a cottage to shelter the family, no cottager would have been reduced to the last degree of penury.

The industrious population which inhabit towns have still fewer data than those of the country, for calculating the lot of the succeeding generation. The workman knows only that he has lived by his labour; he naturally believes that his children will do so likewise. How can he judge of the extent of the market, or the general demand for labour in his country, whilst the master who employs him is incessantly mistaken on these points? Accordingly, this class, more dependent than any other on chances of every kind for its subsistence, is exactly the class which calculates those chances least in the formation of a family. They are the people who marry soonest, produce most children, and consequently lose most: but they do not lose their children, till after being themselves exposed to a competition which deprives them successively of all the sweets of life.

At the time when all towns were distributed into bodies of tradesmen, when a calling could not be exercised till the applicant had been united to a corporation, a workman never married till after he had been passed master. A reception into the trade gave him the certainty of being able to maintain his family; an excessive competition did not expose the great mass of the population to the danger of dying from hunger. Thus, all the institutions created in the republics of the middle ages, and reproduced in Queen Elizabeth's statute of apprenticeship, though keenly attacked by Adam Smith, for establishing a monopoly contrary to the consumer's interest, may be defended, not in regard to the increase of riches, but as forming a necessary obstacle to the immoderate increase of population.

Yet because the system we follow has made us experience a calamity, we ought not to imagine that no escape is to be found, except by rushing into the opposite extreme. It is not by the suppression of corporations alone, that we have disproportionately increased the manufacturing population. It is much more by the inordinate encouragement which all governments, at the same time, have given to production without attending to consumption. We have already pointed out the results of this imprudent struggle, in regard to the increase of wealth. They have been still more disastrous in producing and supporting with deceitful hopes a population, which has afterwards been abandoned to all the horrors of want.

A state ought, doubtless, to receive with gratitude whatever new industry the wants of consumers may develop but it also ought to allow the industry which is quitting it to depart, without any effort to the contrary. When the profits of a manufacture diminish, new workmen do not engage in it; former workmen withdraw; and after some years of suffering, too long and too cruel, by any mode of treatment, the level is again established. But if the favours of government keep up the staggering manufacture; if, trying to save it, government offers bounties for the discovery of any machine which shall spare manual labour, it will prolong suffering, and save the manufacturer only at the expense of those whom that manufacturer should support.

The guardian population presents the same species of suffering in another rank of society. War multiplies the commissions of officers in the army and navy; the complicacy of administration multiplies the places of judges and civil agents of all kinds. Religious zeal multiplies the places for pastors. All of them live on pensions with a certain degree of opulence; none of them knows, or is able to insure the fund which affords him subsistence. They reckon on ushering their children into the same career with themselves; they bring them up, multiply their families in proportion to their actual opulence, and blindly repose on the future. Their pension, however, finishes with their life; and at death they leave their children in a state of indigence, the suffering of which is farther aggravated by the possession of a liberal education. The laws which obstruct the marriage of officers, judges, clergymen, and generally of all such as live on pensions, how hard soever those law may appear at their first establishment, are justifiable, because they save from poverty the class to which its torments would be most piercing.

But an inordinate increase of population is not the only cause of this national suffering. The demand for labour may decrease, and the population continue stationary. Consumption may be arrested, revenues dissipated, capital destroyed, and the number of hands formerly occupied may no longer be able to find a sufficient employment. The population immediately follow the revolution of the capitals destined to support it. As day-labourers are more eager to receive even the smallest wage, than merchants to employ their money, the former are laid under conditions more and more hard, as the demand on the capital diminishes; and they conclude by contenting themselves with so miserable a remuneration, as is scarcely sufficient to maintain them alive. No enjoyment is any longer attached to the existence of this unhappy class; hunger and suffering stifle in them all the moral affections. When every hour is a struggle for life, all passions are concentrated in selfishness; each forgets the pain of others in what himself suffers; the sentiments of nature are blunted; a constant, obstinate, uniform labour, debases all the faculties. One blushes for the human species, to see how low on the scale of degradation it can descend; how much beneath the condition of animals it can voluntarily submit to maintain life; and, notwithstanding all the benefits of social order, notwithstanding the advantages which man has gained from the arts, one is sometimes tempted to execrate the division of labour, and the invention of manufactures on beholding to what extremes of wretchedness they have reduced beings created equal with ourselves.

The misery of the savage hunter, who dies so frequently of hunger, is not equal to that of millions of families, whom a manufacturer sometimes dismisses; because at least there remains to the former, all the energy, and all the intelligence, which he has put to proof during all his life. When he dies for want of finding game, he yields to a necessity which nature herself presents, and to which he knew, from the beginning, he must submit, as to sickness, or to old age. But the artisan, dismissed from his workshop, with his wife and children, has beforehand lost the strength of his soul and his body; he is still surrounded with riches; he still sees beside him, at every step, the food which he requires; and if society refuses him the labour by which he offers, till his last moment, to purchase bread, it is men, not nature, that he blames.

Even when persons do not actually die of hunger; even when the aids of charity are eagerly administered to all indigent families, discouragement and suffering produce their cruel effects on the poor, the diseases of the soul are communicated to the body, epidemics are multiplied, children die in a few months after their birth, and the suppression of labour causes more cruel ravages than the cruellest war: besides, fatal habits, either of mendicity or idleness, take root in the population; another course is given to trade, another direction to fashion, and even after death has cleared the ranks of workmen, those who remain are no longer in a condition to support the competition of foreigners.

The causes of diminution in the demand for labour, often belong to polity, properly so called, rather than to political economy. There is, perhaps, none more efficacious than the loss or diminution of liberty, When a nation begins to alienate this precious possession, each citizen thinks himself less secure of his fortune, of the fruits of his labour; each abates something of the activity of his mind, and his spirit of industry. The virtues which accompany labour, - sobriety, constancy, economy - give place to the vices of idleness, to intemperance, dissipation, and forgetfulness of the future. Trade, industry, activity, are regarded with contempt, in a state where the people are nothing, whilst all distinction, all honours, are reserved for noble indolence. Favour, intrigue, flattery, and all the arts of courtiers, which debase the soul, are roads to fortune, much more sure and rapid than strength of character, bold and enterprising activity, or a spirit of speculation. Intriguers are multiplied daily; they regard with contempt those who follow the only honourable path to fortune, that in which none makes progress except by his merit or his labour.

One cause of depopulation is, however, presented, which lies within the narrowest range of political economy. The progress of the arts, the progress of industry, and hence even that of wealth and prosperity, discover economical methods of producing all the fruits of labour, by employing a smaller number of workmen. Animals are substituted for men in almost all the details of agriculture; and machines are substituted for men in all the operations of manufactures. So long as a nation finds within its reach a market sufficiently extensive to secure for all its productions a prompt and advantageous circulation, each of those discoveries is an advantage, because, instead of diminishing the number of workmen, it augments the mass of labour and its produce. A nation which happens to originate discoveries, succeeds, for a long time, in extending its market in proportion to the number of hands set free by every new invention. It immediately employs them in augmenting the produce, which the discovery promises to furnish at a cheaper rate. But a period arrives at last, when the whole civilized world is but one market, and when new customers cannot be found in new nations. The demand of the universal market is then a precise quantity, which the different industrious nations dispute with each other; if one furnish more, another must furnish less. The total sale can only be increased by the progress of general opulence, or because conveniences, formerly confined to the rich, are brought within the reach of the poor.

The invention of the stocking frame, by means of which one man does as much work as a hundred did before, was a benefit for humanity, only because, at the same time, the progress of civilization, of population, and of wealth, increased the number of consumers. New counties adopted the customs of

138

Europe; and this article of dress, formerly reserved for the rich, has now descended to the poorest classes. But if, at the present day, some new discovery should enable us, by a single stocking-frame, to do the work which ten years ago was done by a hundred, this discovery would be a national misfortune; for the number of consumers can scarcely increase, and it would then be the number of producers which would be diminished.

This example may show us the general rule: Whenever a discovery, economizing labour, brings within the reach of a poorer class what was previously confined to the rich, it extends the market; and whilst benefiting undertakers, and poor consumers, it does no harm to workmen. But when the discovery cannot increase the number of consumers, though it serves them at a cheaper rate, either because they are already all furnished, or because the thing produced can never be useful to them, however low it may fall, - the discovery becomes a human calamity; because it is advantageous but to a certain manufacturer, and that only at the expense of his brethren; or it benefits a single nation, and that only at the expense of others. This national benefit, if purchased at the expense of wretchedness and famine to foreign artisans, would not in itself be much worth coveting; it is, besides, very far from being certain. From the progress of communication between different states, from the skill of manufacturers, a discovery in one country is imitated in every other before the former has gained any great profit from it.

It will doubtless be said, that whoever introduces a saving in any article of his consumption, preserving still the same revenue, will consume what he saves from the fall of price in such and such an article, by a new expenditure, for which he will put in requisition a new labour. But there never will be any proportion between this new demand and the labour suspended on account of it.

On one hand, consumers make use of goods a little finer, a little prettier, at the same price. The clothes with which the poor workman is dressed, are a little superior in quality, are really worth a little more than those which covered his father, at the expense of the same part of his wages. But himself does not perceive this advantage. Decency, which according to this station, he is obliged to consult, leaves him no choice; he must dress like his equals, without finding more enjoyment; he makes no saving in this article, he cannot apply it to any other expense.

On the other hand, the price of goods is not always established in direct proportion to the labour they require, but in a very complicated proportion subsisting between this annual labour, the circulating capital, and a primary, unrenewed labour, consumed in building the manufactory, constructing the machinery with expensive and often foreign materials. Hence, even when a hundred workmen are dismissed, that the work may be done with one by means of machinery,the goods are not reduced to the hundredth part of their price. The stocking-frame economizes work nearly in this proportion, yet it scarcely produces stockings ten per cent. cheaper than those made with the needle. Notwithstanding the invention of large mills for spinning wool, silk, cotton, women continue to be employed in spinning with the wheel, or even with the distaff; a certain proof that the saving does not exceed ten per cent. The same observation may be extended to all improved manufactures: they have never diminished the price of their produce, except in arithmetical progression, while they have suspended workmanship in geometrical progression.

Let us compare this saving in workmanship with the saving in price, according to the most simple calculation on the commonest manufacture. A hundred thousand women, who knit with the needle each a hundred pair of stockings annually, produce ten million pairs; which, at 5s. a-piece, would sell at 2,500,000 l.: the raw material is worth a fifth of this. There remains 2,000,000 to distribute among 100,000 workmen, or 20 l. a-head.

The same work is done at present on the frame by 1000

workmen, and comes in ten per cent. cheaper, at 4s. 6d. a pair, or, 2,250,000 l. In all the nation therefore saves 250,000 l. If employed solely in workmanship, this sum would be sufficient to maintain 12,500 of the workers who have been dismissed. But this is not what happens; the consumer, accustomed to buy stockings at 5s. a pair, pays still the same price; but, by reason of the progress of the art, he merely wears them a little finer. This progress in his luxury gives subsistence to a tenth more stocking manufactures, that is to a hundred more; to these add still farther a hundred workmen employed in repairing the machines, or constructing new ones, and you have in all 1200 workmen living on the sum which supported 100,000.

The same calculation is applicable to all improved manufactures; for the manufacturer, in adopting a new machine, and dismissing his workmen, never troubles himself with inquiring whether he shall make a profit equal to the diminution of workmanship, but merely whether he shall be enabled to sell a little cheaper than his rivals. All the workmen of England would be turned to the street, if the manufacturers could employ steam engines in their place, with a saving of five per cent.

Besides, the improvement of machinery, and the economy of human labour, contribute immediately to diminish the number of national consumers; for all the ruined workmen were consumers. In the country. the introduction of the large farming system has banished from Great Britain the class of peasant farmers, who laboured themselves, and yet enjoyed an honest plenty. The population has been considerably diminished, but its consumption is reduced still farther than its number. The hinds perform all sorts of field labour, are limited to the scantiest necessaries, and give not nearly so much encouragement to the industry of towns as the rich peasants gave before.

A similar change has taken place in the population of towns. Discoveries in the mechanical arts have always the remote result of concentrating industry within the hands of a smaller number of richer merchants. They enable men to perform with an expensive machine, that is to say, with great capital, what was formerly performed with a great labour. They discover the economy which exists in management on a great scale, the division of operation, the employment common to a great number of men at once, of light, fuel, and all the powers of nature. Thus small merchants, small manufacturers disappear; and our great undertaker supplies the place of hundreds, who, all together, perhaps, were not as rich as he. All together were, however, better consumers than he. His expensive luxury gives far less encouragement to industry than the honest plenty of a hundred households, of which his household supplies the place.

As even new demands made manufactures prosper, the number of labourers, in spite of the augmented powers of labour, increases likewise; and such as were dismissed from the country found still an establishment in manufacturing towns, the population of which continued to increase. But now when at last the market of the universe has been found sufficiently provided for, and new reductions of workmen have occurred; when hinds have been dismissed from the fields, spinners from the manufactories of cotton, weavers from those of cloth; when each day a new machine supplies the place of several families, whilst no new demand offers them an occupation or a livelihood; distress has reached its height, and one might begin to regret the progress of this civilization, which, by collecting a greater number of individuals in the same space of ground, has but multiplied their wretchedness, whilst in deserts it could at least but reach a small number of victims. One might also regret that governments have studied too late, and neglected too constantly the precepts of a science, which, teaching the origin of national prosperity, points out beforehand its danger, and the causes of its destruction.

www.ingramcontent.com/pod-product-compliance
Lightning Source LLC
Chambersburg PA
CBHW051349280526
45784CB00007B/2884